BLOOM

Founded by | arihant

Olympiad ACE

A Comprehensive Practice Book

for School Olympiads & Talent Search Exams

GENERAL KNOWLEDGE

Class 5

by

Suman Bharti

Olympiad ACE

BLOOM

Bloom Cap Edu Ventures Pvt. Ltd.

卐 **Administrative & Production Office**

'Ramchhaya' 4577/15, Agarwal Road, Darya Ganj, New Delhi -110002
Tele: 011- 47630600, 43518550

卐 **PRICE:** ₹125.00

卐 PO No. : TXT-59-T067224-09-25

Published by Arihant Publications (I) Ltd.

For further information about the books log on to
www.bloomcap.org

Follow us on

Preface

"Future belongs to those Who prepares for it today"

School Olympiads are National & International level competitions conducted by different Government, Non-Government & Educational Organisations with the purpose of making the children ready to face competitive exams. The challenging Questions asked in Olympiads motivate them to learn more & more and bring out the best result with improved academic performance. The Awards & Scholarship offered by Olympiads motivate children to aspire & strive for doing better and emerge out to be the best.

GK Olympiads

GK is the knowledge of every aspect of the human life, which may or may not be the part of routine academic studies but very important for the overall personality development of the students. It is more or less connected with the attentiveness and awareness. There can be different domains of GK like; History, Geography, Polity, Culture, Discovery, Sports, Current Affairs etc.

GK Olympiads help students in understanding the importance of General Knowledge and updations about National & International Affairs in daily life.

'Bloom GK Olympiad Study Book Class 5' is a perfect resource to Study & Practice for Olympiad Exams and other National & State Level Talent Search Exams & Other Competitions.

Some Special Features of Bloom GK Olympiad Study Books are;

- Complete coverage of all the topics related to GK;. History, Geography, Environment, Polity, Science, Sports, etc.
- Chapterwise Exercises having different types of Objective Questions.
- Olympiad Pattern Practice Sets at the end.

This book is prepared by Expert Panel with the utmost care, still if you have any suggestions regarding its improvement then feel free to contact us at support@bloomcap.org. We will try to inculcate your suggestions in the further editions.

Contents

01

History of India

MCQs 1 Mark Questions

1. Who among the following was the founder of the Mauryan Empire?
(a) Akbar
(b) Ashoka
(c) Chandragupta I
(d) Porus

2. The famous Sanchi Stupa in Madhya Pradesh was built by the Great Mauryan Emperor who is known as ....
(a) Ashoka
(b) Akbar
(c) Maharana Pratap
(d) Shah Jahan

3. Name the ruler from among the following who was the son of Emperor Babur.
(a) Akbar
(b) Humayun
(c) Shah Jahan
(d) Aurangzeb

4. Which among the following structures was/were built during the reign of Akbar?
(a) Fatehpur Sikri
(b) Buland Darwaza
(c) Agra Fort
(d) All of these

5. Name the freedom fighter that is also called 'Punjab Kesari' and 'Lion of Punjab'.
(a) Chandra Shekhar Azad
(b) Lala Lajpat Rai
(c) Sardar Vallabhbhai Patel
(d) Mahatma Gandhi

6. General Dyer is associated with which of the following events?
(a) Revolt of 1857
(b) Jallianwala Bagh Massacre
(c) Partition of Bengal
(d) Kakori Conspiracy Case

7. Identify from the pictures given below, the freedom fighter of 1857 revolt who was an Indian soldier in the British army.

(a) 

(b) 

(c) 

(d) 

8. Unscramble the group of letters to find out the name of the person with the help of information given below.

Name the ruler who is considered as the founder of the Maratha Empire.

(a) RAOBAJI (b) VAJISHI (c) OKAASH (d) HWAPES

9. Identify the incorrectly matched pair.

(a) Bhagat Singh – Shaheed-e-Azam
(b) Bipin Chandra Pal – Pal in 'Lal-Bal-Pal'
(c) Gopal Krishna Gokhale – Gold of India
(d) Bal Gangadhar Tilak – Lokmanya

10. Which among the following leaders started the Non-Cooperation Movement?

(a) Jawaharlal Nehru (b) Bal Gangadhar Tilak
(c) Mahatma Gandhi (d) Lala Lajpat Rai

11. The first nationalist freedom fighter who brought the concept of 'Swaraj' was ....

(a) Subhash Chandra Bose (b) Bal Gangadhar Tilak
(c) Jawaharlal Nehru (d) Bipin Chandra Pal

12. Who is popularly known as Father of Indian Renaissance?

(a) Mahatma Phule (b) MG Ranade
(c) Raja Ram Mohan Roy (d) Dayanand Saraswati

13. Identify the leader who led the Azad Hind Fauz and fought for India's freedom.

(a) Netaji Subhash Chandra Bose (b) Sardar Vallabhbhai Patel
(c) Mahatma Gandhi (d) None of these

14. **Complete the given analogy.**

Nightingale of India : Sarojini Naidu :: Iron Man of India : ?

(a) Jawaharlal Nehru (b) Sardar Vallabhbhai Patel
(c) Mahatma Gandhi (d) Subhash Chandra Bose

15. **Identify the freedom struggle leader, who is shown in the picture given below.**

(a) Bal Gangadhar Tilak (b) Deshbandhu Chittranjan Das
(c) Lala Lajpat Rai (d) Sardar Vallabhbhai Patel

16. **Name the personality who is credited with the establishment of Aligarh Muslim University.**

(a) Sir Syed Ahmed Khan (b) Aga Khan
(c) Abbas Ali (d) Muzaffar Ahmed

17. **Who among the following was the freedom fighter who became the second Prime Minister of India and gave the slogan 'Jai Jawan Jai Kisan'.**

(a) Bhagat Singh (b) Jawaharlal Nehru
(c) Lal Bahadur Shastri (d) Sarvepalli Radhakrishnan

MCQs 2 Marks Questions

18. **Match the following.**

List I (Freedom Fighters)	**List II** (Slogans)
A. Bhagat Singh	1. Give me blood and I will give you freedom
B. Netaji Subhash Chandra Bose	2. Inquilab Zindabad
C. Mahatma Gandhi	3. Swaraj is my birthright and I will have it
D. Bal Gangadhar Tilak	4. Do or Die

Codes

	A	B	C	D		A	B	C	D
(a)	1	2	3	4	(b)	4	1	2	3
(c)	2	1	4	3	(d)	3	1	2	4

19. Read the given statements and select the correct option.

I. Birbal was one of the Navratna in Akbar's court.

II. Akbar was one of the greatest monarches of the Mughal dynasty.

Codes

(a) Only I (b) Only II

(c) Both I and II (d) Neither I nor II

20. On the basis of facts, some statements given below are true or false, find which ones are true (T) and which ones are false (F).

I. Vinoba Bhave was considered as National Teacher of India and the spiritual successor of Mahatma Gandhi.

II. Mahatma Gandhi launched the Non-Cooperation Movement in 1920.

III. Poona Pact was signed between Mahatma Gandhi and Dr BR Ambedkar.

Codes

	I	II	III
(a)	F	F	T
(b)	T	T	T
(c)	F	T	F
(d)	T	T	F

21. Identify the personality with the help of information given below.

- I am known for raising my voice against the injustice caused to untouchables.
- I was a lawyer by profession and was popularly known as Baba Saheb.

(a) Jawaharlal Nehru (b) Mahatma Gandhi

(c) BR Ambedkar (d) GK Gokhale

Darken your choice with HB Pencil

1.	ⓐ ⓑ ⓒ ⓓ	5.	ⓐ ⓑ ⓒ ⓓ	9.	ⓐ ⓑ ⓒ ⓓ	13.	ⓐ ⓑ ⓒ ⓓ	17.	ⓐ ⓑ ⓒ ⓓ	21.	ⓐ ⓑ ⓒ ⓓ
2.	ⓐ ⓑ ⓒ ⓓ	6.	ⓐ ⓑ ⓒ ⓓ	10.	ⓐ ⓑ ⓒ ⓓ	14.	ⓐ ⓑ ⓒ ⓓ	18.	ⓐ ⓑ ⓒ ⓓ		
3.	ⓐ ⓑ ⓒ ⓓ	7.	ⓐ ⓑ ⓒ ⓓ	11.	ⓐ ⓑ ⓒ ⓓ	15.	ⓐ ⓑ ⓒ ⓓ	19.	ⓐ ⓑ ⓒ ⓓ		
4.	ⓐ ⓑ ⓒ ⓓ	8.	ⓐ ⓑ ⓒ ⓓ	12.	ⓐ ⓑ ⓒ ⓓ	16.	ⓐ ⓑ ⓒ ⓓ	20.	ⓐ ⓑ ⓒ ⓓ		

02

Art and Culture

MCQs 1 Mark Questions

1. The famous play dance 'Raslila' belongs to which of the following states?

(a) Haryana (b) Uttar Pradesh (c) Gujarat (d) Tamil Nadu

2. Name the annual fair of Rajasthan that is famous for its cattle trading event.

(a) Pushkar Mela (b) Kumbh Mela
(c) Surajkund Mela (d) Ganga Sagar Mela

3. Which Indian academy promotes dance, drama and music?

(a) Sahitya Academy (b) Lalit Kala Academy
(c) Sangeet Academy (d) National School of Drama

4. Choose the classical dance that is famous in the state of Assam.

(a) Sattriya (b) Kuchipudi (c) Bhangra (d) Garba

5. Identify the incorrectly matched pair.

States		Festivals
(a) Assam	–	Bihu
(b) Maharashtra	–	Ganesh Chaturthi
(c) Gujarat	–	Durga Puja
(d) Rajasthan	–	Gangaur

6. Identify the instrument which was invented by Amir Khusrau.

(a) Veena (b) Sitar (c) Tabla (d) Harmonium

7. Boat races are conducted during the festival of ....

(a) Pongal (b) Onam (c) Bihu (d) Holi

8. Complete the given analogy.

Pithora painting : Gujarat :: Madhubani painting : ?

(a) Assam (b) Bihar (c) Odisha (d) West Bengal

9. **In which of the following styles of dance, the story/ theme is always taken from Mahabharata and Ramayana?**

(a) Bharatnatyam (b) Mohiniyattam (c) Kuchipudi (d) Kathak

10. **Who among the following is referred to as the 'Parrot of India'?**

(a) Amir Khusrau (b) Mirza Ghalib (c) Tansen (d) Sarojini Naidu

11. **Identify the given pictures and choose the one that is representing Manipuri dance form.**

(a) 

(b) 

(c) 

(d) None of these

12. **Which Indian state hosts the famous 'Khajuraho Dance Festival'?**

(a) Odisha (b) West Bengal (c) Madhya Pradesh (d) Chhattisgarh

13. **Unscramble the group of letters to find out the name of the state with the help of information given below.**

The famous Chhau Festival belongs to this state.

(a) SHAODI (b) THANRAJAS (c) AMASS (d) HARBI

14. **'Theyyam' or 'Kaliyattam' is a ritual dance performed in which State/UT?**

(a) Karnataka (b) Kerala
(c) Andhra Pradesh (d) West Bengal

MCQs 2 Marks Questions

15. **Read the given statements and select the correct option.**

I. Konark Festival is celebrated in the state of Odisha.

II. Losoong Festival is celebrated in the state of Sikkim.

Codes

(a) Only I (b) Only II (c) Both I and II (d) Neither I nor II

16. **Match the following.**

List I	List II
A. Khandoba	1. Rajasthan
B. Hornbill Festival	2. Maharashtra
C. Baikho	3. Assam
D. Mewar Festival	4. Nagaland

Codes

	A	B	C	D		A	B	C	D
(a)	1	2	3	4	(b)	4	1	2	3
(c)	2	4	3	1	(d)	3	1	2	4

17. **On the basis of facts, some statements given below are true or false, find which ones are true (T) and which ones are false (F).**

I. Bhangra is the folk dance popular during the harvest season in Punjab.

II. Flamingo Festival is celebrated in the state of Andhra Pradesh.

III. Rukmini Devi is a famous dancer of Bharatnatyam dance form.

Codes

	I	II	III		I	II	III
(a)	F	F	T	(b)	T	T	T
(c)	F	T	F	(d)	T	T	F

18. **Identify the following with the help of information given below.**

- **I am the classical music of Northern regions of the Indian sub-continent.**
- **I am played along with the instruments like the violin, sitar and sarod.**

(a) Hindustani Classical Music (b) Carnatic Music

(c) Western Pop (d) Opera

Darken your choice with HB Pencil

1.	ⓐ ⓑ ⓒ ⓓ	4.	ⓐ ⓑ ⓒ ⓓ	7.	ⓐ ⓑ ⓒ ⓓ	10.	ⓐ ⓑ ⓒ ⓓ	13.	ⓐ ⓑ ⓒ ⓓ	16.	ⓐ ⓑ ⓒ ⓓ
2.	ⓐ ⓑ ⓒ ⓓ	5.	ⓐ ⓑ ⓒ ⓓ	8.	ⓐ ⓑ ⓒ ⓓ	11.	ⓐ ⓑ ⓒ ⓓ	14.	ⓐ ⓑ ⓒ ⓓ	17.	ⓐ ⓑ ⓒ ⓓ
3.	ⓐ ⓑ ⓒ ⓓ	6.	ⓐ ⓑ ⓒ ⓓ	9.	ⓐ ⓑ ⓒ ⓓ	12.	ⓐ ⓑ ⓒ ⓓ	15.	ⓐ ⓑ ⓒ ⓓ	18.	ⓐ ⓑ ⓒ ⓓ

03

Indian Architecture

MCQs 1 Mark Questions

1. **Which of the following is the ancient seat of learning situated in the state of Bihar?**

(a) Taxila (b) Nalanda
(c) Vikramshila (d) Vallabhi

2. **Choose the building that is known as the 'White Marble Mughal Architecture'.**

(a) Taj Mahal (b) Qutub Minar
(c) Charminar Fort (d) Ajanta

3. **What is the name of the tallest brick and stone minarets located in New Delhi?**

(a) Taj Mahal (b) Qutub Minar
(c) Jama Masjid (d) Humayun's Tomb

Which heritage site is well known for its stepped corridors, sculptures and stone carvings in the well?

(a) Fatehpur Sikri (b) Rani ki Vav
(c) Sun Temple (d) None of these

5. **Identify the name of the India's largest and oldest museum.**

(a) Indian Museum, Kolkata (b) National Museum, New Delhi
(c) National Rail Museum, New Delhi (d) Assam State Museum, Guwahati

6. **The 'Statue of Unity' known as the tallest statue in the world is located in ....**

(a) Rajasthan (b) New Delhi
(c) Gujarat (d) Bihar

7. **Choose among the options, the fort that is known as the 'Great Wall of India' located in Rajasthan.**

(a) Jaisalmer Fort (b) Kumbhalgarh Fort
(c) Humayun's Tomb (d) Fatehpur Sikri

8. **Identify the incorrectly matched pair.**
(a) Gateway of India – Mumbai
(b) Gol Gumbaz – Bijapur
(c) Bibi Ka Maqbara – Nasik
(d) Hawa Mahal – Jaipur

9. **Which of the following is the oldest stone structure in India?**
(a) Sanchi Stupa (b) Red Fort
(c) Vijaya Stambh (d) None of these

10. **The given picture is of Bhubaneshwar Temple which is located in the state of ... .**

(a) Rajasthan (b) Odisha
(c) Gujarat (d) Tamil Nadu

11. **Complete the given analogy.**
Cellular Jail : Andaman :: Vivekananda Rock : ?
(a) Jaipur (b) Kanyakumari
(c) Srinagar (d) Patna

12. **Choose from the given options, one of the 'oldest churches' in India that is also a world heritage site located in Goa.**
(a) Santa Cruz Basilica (b) Basilica of Bom Jesus
(c) St Francis Church (d) St Paul Cathedral

13. **Which of the famous temple town is known for the Ratha Temples?**
(a) Mahabalipuram (b) Kolkata (c) Puri (d) None of these

14. **Name one of the most 'Haunted Fort' in India that is located in Rajasthan.**
(a) Bhangarh Fort (b) Mehrangarh Fort
(c) Jaisalmer Fort (d) None of these

15. Identify the given pictures and choose the one that is one of the world's most beautiful religious buildings in Delhi.

(a) 

(b) 

(c) 

(d) None of these

16. .... is also known as the 'Diamond of Kollur Mine' and is located in Hyderabad.

(a) Golconda Fort (b) Kumbhalgarh Fort
(c) Jaisalmer Fort (d) Agra Fort

17. Which of the following is the 'First Garden Tomb' built in India?

(a) Humayun's Tomb (b) Bibi Ka Maqbara
(c) Purana Qila (d) Akbar's Tomb

18. Name the place which was earlier known as the 'Victoria Terminus'.

(a) Hazrat Nizamuddin Terminus (b) Bandra Terminus
(c) Allahabad Junction (d) Chhatrapati Shivaji Terminus

19. Which of the following monuments is known as the 'Tower of Fame'?

(a) Qutub Minar (b) Kirti Stambh (c) Deep Stambh (d) Rajput Stambh

20. 'Statue of Peace' is located in which of the following states?

(a) Rajasthan (b) Madhya Pradesh
(c) Gujarat (d) Karnataka

MCQs 2 Marks Questions

21. Match the following.

List I (Modern Architecture)	List II (Location)
A. Shore Temple	1. Agra
B. Fatehpur Sikri	2. Hyderabad
C. Mecca Masjid	3. Rajasthan
D. Dilwara Jain Temple	4. Mahabalipuram

Codes

	A	B	C	D		A	B	C	D
(a)	1	2	3	4	(b)	4	1	2	3
(c)	2	4	3	1	(d)	3	1	2	4

22. Read the given statements and select the correct option.

I. Kailasha Temple is the largest of rock-cut Hindu temples at the Ellora caves.

II. Gateway of India is also known as the Taj Mahal of Delhi.

Codes

(a) Only I (b) Only II
(c) Both I and II (d) Neither I nor II

23. On the basis of facts, some statements given below are true or false, find which ones are true (T) and which ones are false (F).

I. Chittorgarh Fort is the largest fort in India and a World Heritage Site.

II. Agra Fort is located in Uttar Pradesh and was built by Lodhis.

III. Agrasen Ki Baoli is the oldest monument of Central Delhi, one of the most preserved Baolis of the city.

Codes

	I	II	III
(a)	F	F	T
(b)	T	F	T
(c)	F	T	F
(d)	T	T	F

24. Identify the following with the help of information given below.

- **I am one of the most magnificent structures in Lucknow.**
- **It is an important place of worship for Shia Muslims.**

(a) Bara Imambara (b) Moti Masjid
(c) Chota Imambara (d) Sheesh Mahal

Darken your choice with HB Pencil

1. ⓐ ⓑ ⓒ ⓓ	5. ⓐ ⓑ ⓒ ⓓ	9. ⓐ ⓑ ⓒ ⓓ	13. ⓐ ⓑ ⓒ ⓓ	17. ⓐ ⓑ ⓒ ⓓ	21. ⓐ ⓑ ⓒ ⓓ
2. ⓐ ⓑ ⓒ ⓓ	6. ⓐ ⓑ ⓒ ⓓ	10. ⓐ ⓑ ⓒ ⓓ	14. ⓐ ⓑ ⓒ ⓓ	18. ⓐ ⓑ ⓒ ⓓ	22. ⓐ ⓑ ⓒ ⓓ
3. ⓐ ⓑ ⓒ ⓓ	7. ⓐ ⓑ ⓒ ⓓ	11. ⓐ ⓑ ⓒ ⓓ	15. ⓐ ⓑ ⓒ ⓓ	19. ⓐ ⓑ ⓒ ⓓ	23. ⓐ ⓑ ⓒ ⓓ
4. ⓐ ⓑ ⓒ ⓓ	8. ⓐ ⓑ ⓒ ⓓ	12. ⓐ ⓑ ⓒ ⓓ	16. ⓐ ⓑ ⓒ ⓓ	20. ⓐ ⓑ ⓒ ⓓ	24. ⓐ ⓑ ⓒ ⓓ

04

Our Universe

MCQs 1 Mark Questions

1. What is the path along which planet revolve around the Sun called ?
   (a) Axis (b) Orbit (c) Circle (d) None of these

2. Name the planets that have no natural satellites or Moon.
   (a) Mars and Jupiter (b) Mercury and Venus
   (c) Uranus and Mars (d) Mars and Venus

3. A group of stars that form a beautiful pattern is known as ....
   (a) comets (b) asteroids (c) constellations (d) meteoroids

4. Which of the following are also known as small planets or planetoids largely found between Mars and Jupiter?
   (a) Comets (b) Meteors (c) Asteroids (d) None of these

5. Identify the incorrectly matched pair.
   (a) Inner Planet – Earth
   (b) Outer Planet – Saturn
   (c) Morning Star – Venus
   (d) Ringed Planet – Jupiter

6. Name the planet that rotates in an opposite direction to that of the Earth.
   (a) Mercury (b) Venus
   (c) Jupiter (d) Neptune

7. Which of the following heavenly bodies is made up of millions of stars?
   (a) Sun (b) Black Hole
   (c) Galaxy (d) Solar System

8. Name the planet that has a lesser rotation time than the Earth.
   (a) Jupiter (b) Mercury
   (c) Mars (d) Venus

9. .... is an imaginary line which divides the Earth into Eastern and Western Hemisphere.
(a) Equator (b) Prime Meridian
(c) Tropic of Cancer (d) Latitude

10. The Earth rotates in which direction on its axis?
(a) North to South (b) West to East
(c) East to West (d) South to North

11. Complete the given analogy.
Moon : Revolves around the Earth :: Mars : ?
(a) Revolves around the Sun (b) Rotates around the Sun
(c) Revolves around Neptune (d) None of these

12. Choose the correct order of planets from the Sun.
(a) Mercury, Venus, Earth, Mars, Jupiter
(b) Mars, Venus, Earth, Jupiter, Mercury
(c) Jupiter, Mercury, Venus, Mars, Earth
(d) Venus, Mercury, Mars, Jupiter, Earth

13. How many days does the Moon require to complete its one revolution around the Earth?
(a) 27 (b) 64
(c) 31 (d) 30

14. Identify the given pictures and choose the Orion constellation.

(a) 

(b) 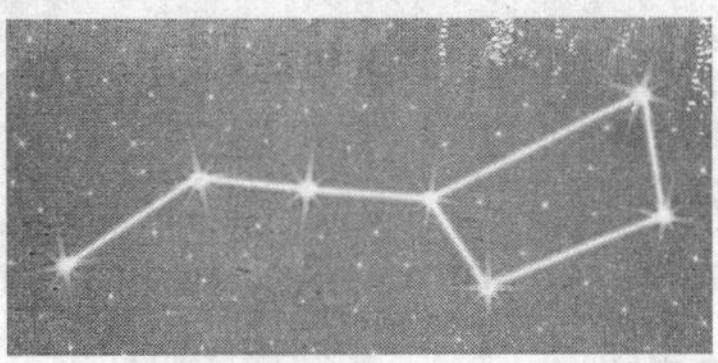

(c) 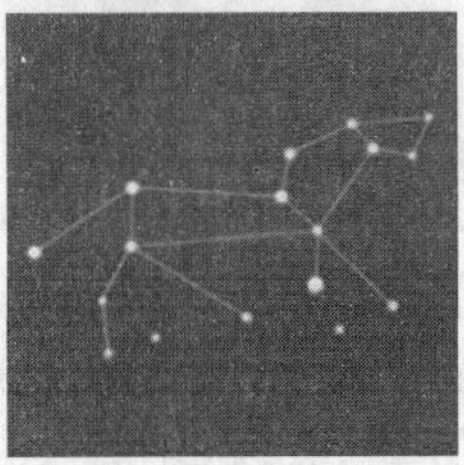

(d) None of these

15. **Identify from the image given below, which is popular as 'Shooting Stars' and can normally be seen in the upper atmosphere.**

(a) Comets b) Meteors (c) Asteroids (d) Orbit

16. **How many days does the Earth take to complete its one revolution around the Sun?**

(a) 244 days (b) 270 days (c) 300 days (d) 365 days

17. **Unscramble the group of letters to find out the name with the help of information given below.**

The movement of the Earth that is responsible for light and darkness.

(a) UTIONREVOL (b) TIONROTA
(c) TONICTEC (d) MENTMOVE

18. **Identify the imaginary line that divides the Earth into two equal halves.**

(a) Equator (b) Meridian
(c) Tropic of Cancer (d) Longitude

19. **Which of the following is the shape of the Earth?**

(a) Circular (b) Elliptical (c) Rectangular (d) Semi-circular

20. **Leap year is repeated after how many years?**

(a) Two years (b) Three years
(c) Four years (d) Five years

21. **What is the period between day and night called?**

(a) Axis (b) Orbit (c) Dusk (d) Dawn

22. **Identify the planets that are on either side of the Earth.**

(a) Mercury and Venus (b) Mars and Jupiter
(c) Mars and Venus (d) Venus and Saturn

23. **In which of the following conditions can a lunar eclipse be seen?**

(a) Half Moon (b) Full Moon
(c) New Moon (d) Crescent Moon

24. **Name the planet that is also known as the Sleeping Planet.**

(a) Mars (b) Neptune
(c) Earth (d) Mercury

25. **In how many days can the Full Moon be seen from the naked eyes?**

(a) 12 days (b) 15 days
(c) 29.5 days (d) 16 days

26. **Identify the Crescent Moon from the different forms of Moon shown in the images given below.**

(a) 

(b) 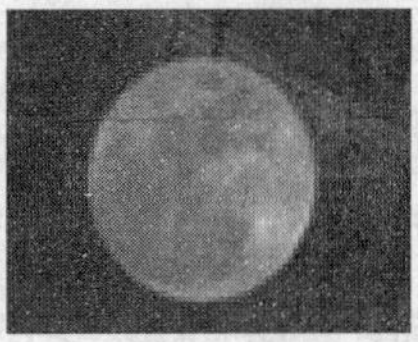

(c) 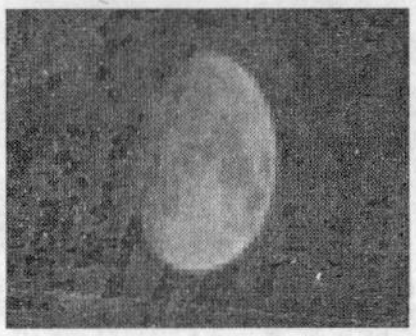

(d) None of these

MCQs 2 Marks Questions

27. **Match the following.**

List I	List II
A. Saturn	1. Largest planet
B. Jupiter	2. Last planet
C. Neptune	3. Nearest planet to the Sun
D. Mercury	4. Second largest planet

Codes

	A	B	C	D
(a)	1	2	3	4
(b)	4	1	2	3
(c)	2	4	3	1
(d)	2	1	4	3

28. Read the given statements and select the correct option.

I. The outermost layer of the Sun is called Corona.

II. The Sun is the only star in the Milky Way Galaxy.

Codes

(a) Only I (b) Only II (c) Both I and II (d) Neither I nor II

29. On the basis of facts, some statements given below are true or false, find which ones are true (T) and which ones are false (F).

I. Saturn is popular for its spectacular ring system.

II. Mercury is the hottest planet in the Solar System.

Codes

	I	II		I	II
(a)	F	F	(b)	T	T
(c)	F	T	(d)	T	F

30. Identify the following with the help of information given below.

- I revolve around the Sun.
- I am also the name of the only metal on the Earth that is liquid at room temperature.

(a) Mars (b) Mercury (c) Jupiter (d) None of these

31. On the basis of facts, some statements given below are true or false, find which ones are true (T) and which ones are false (F).

I. Stars are celestial bodies that continuously emit light and heat.

II. The Sun is the only star in the Solar System.

III. Stars are not visible from the naked eyes.

Codes

	I	II	III		I	II	III
(a)	F	F	T	(b)	T	T	F
(c)	F	T	F	(d)	T	F	F

Darken your choice with HB Pencil

1. ⓐ ⓑ ⓒ ⓓ	7. ⓐ ⓑ ⓒ ⓓ	13. ⓐ ⓑ ⓒ ⓓ	19. ⓐ ⓑ ⓒ ⓓ	25. ⓐ ⓑ ⓒ ⓓ	31. ⓐ ⓑ ⓒ ⓓ
2. ⓐ ⓑ ⓒ ⓓ	8. ⓐ ⓑ ⓒ ⓓ	14. ⓐ ⓑ ⓒ ⓓ	20. ⓐ ⓑ ⓒ ⓓ	26. ⓐ ⓑ ⓒ ⓓ	
3. ⓐ ⓑ ⓒ ⓓ	9. ⓐ ⓑ ⓒ ⓓ	15. ⓐ ⓑ ⓒ ⓓ	21. ⓐ ⓑ ⓒ ⓓ	27. ⓐ ⓑ ⓒ ⓓ	
4. ⓐ ⓑ ⓒ ⓓ	10. ⓐ ⓑ ⓒ ⓓ	16. ⓐ ⓑ ⓒ ⓓ	22. ⓐ ⓑ ⓒ ⓓ	28. ⓐ ⓑ ⓒ ⓓ	
5. ⓐ ⓑ ⓒ ⓓ	11. ⓐ ⓑ ⓒ ⓓ	17. ⓐ ⓑ ⓒ ⓓ	23. ⓐ ⓑ ⓒ ⓓ	29. ⓐ ⓑ ⓒ ⓓ	
6. ⓐ ⓑ ⓒ ⓓ	12. ⓐ ⓑ ⓒ ⓓ	18. ⓐ ⓑ ⓒ ⓓ	24. ⓐ ⓑ ⓒ ⓓ	30. ⓐ ⓑ ⓒ ⓓ	

05

Important Rivers and Lakes of the World

MCQs 1 Mark Questions

1. Name the river that is also known as the 'National river of India'.
(a) Yamuna (b) Narmada (c) Ganga (d) Brahmaputra

2. In which state of India, Bhagirathi and Alaknanda Rivers combine to form Ganga River?
(a) Assam (b) Uttarakhand (c) Himachal Pradesh (d) Arunachal Pradesh

3. India's highest waterfall 'Jog Falls' is located in …………… .
(a) Maharashtra (b) Madhya Pradesh (c) Karnataka (d) Himachal Pradesh

4. Which of the following is the longest river in the world?
(a) Nile (b) Amazon (c) Yellow River (d) Brahmaputra

5. Identify the name of river on which Howrah Bridge is situated.
(a) Brahmaputra (b) Sutlej (c) Hooghly (d) Yamuna

6. The Bhakra Nangal Dam is the second highest dam which is built on ………… River.
(a) Ganga (b) Yamuna (c) Brahmaputra (d) Sutlej

7. Which of the following is the deepest river in the world?
(a) Amazon (b) Nile (c) Congo (d) Volga

8. Which among the following countries share drainage basin of the river Ganga that drains into the Bay of Bengal?
(a) India (b) Bangladesh (c) Nepal (d) All of these

9. Name the river that carries maximum water into the sea in the world.
(a) Nile (b) Congo (c) Yangtze (d) Amazon

10. **The River Volga that drains into the Caspian Sea flows through which of the following countries?**

(a) USA (b) Russia (c) Germany (d) Finland

11. **Which of the following rivers of India is also known as the Red River?**

(a) Krishna (b) Godavari (c) Brahmaputra (d) Ganga

12. **Name the city that is situated on the banks of Sabarmati River.**

(a) Gandhi Nagar (b) Ahmedabad (c) Pushkar (d) Jaipur

13. **Identify the river(s) that originates from a glacier near the holy Mansarovar Lake.**

(a) Sutlej (b) Indus (c) Brahmaputra (d) All of these

14. **Choose among the following, the world's largest lake that is located in a single country.**

(a) Lake Michigan (b) Lake Victoria (c) Lake Huron (d) None of these

15. **Which among the following is the highest lake in India that is located at a height of 5,430 metres?**

(a) Pushkar Lake (b) Gurudongmar Lake

(c) Chilika Lake (d) Pulicat Lake

16. **Identify the incorrectly matched pair.**

(a) Largest freshwater lake of Asia – Wular Lake

(b) Largest tributary of Ganga – Yamuna

(c) Tallest waterfall in the world – Angel Falls

(d) Largest salt water lake in India – Pulicat Lake

17. **In which State/UT of India is the Pangong Lake situated?**

(a) Ladakh (b) Jammu and Kashmir

(c) Assam (d) Himachal Pradesh

18. **Unscramble the group of letters to find out the name with the help of information given below.**

It is the longest lake in India and located in the state of Rajasthan.

(a) LARWU (b) LIKACHIL (c) LAD (d) KARPUSH

19. **Complete the given analogy.**

World's smallest freshwater lake : Benxi Lake :: World's largest freshwater lake : ?

(a) Lake Superior (b) Caspian Sea (c) Lake Victoria (d) None of these

MCQs 2 Marks Questions

20. **Match the following.**

List I		List II
A. Tungabhadra	1.	Uttarakhand
B. Godavari	2.	Maharashtra
C. Yamuna	3.	Karnataka
D. Indus	4.	Tibet

Codes

	A	B	C	D		A	B	C	D
(a)	1	2	3	4	(b)	3	2	1	4
(c)	2	1	4	3	(d)	4	3	1	2

21. **Read the given statements and select the correct option.**

I. Lake Victoria is a freshwater lake which is located in Africa.

II. Lake Baikal is the deepest lake in the world.

Codes

(a) Only I (b) Only II (c) Both I and II (d) Neither I nor II

22. **On the basis of facts, some statements given below are true or false, find which ones are true (T) and which ones are false (F).**

I. The River Narmada flows through rift valleys and drains into the Arabian Sea.

II. The River Brahmaputra is known as 'Yarlung Tsangpo' in Tibet.

III. Pulicat Lagoon is the second largest brackish water lagoon in India.

Codes

	I	II	III		I	II	III
(a)	F	F	T	(b)	T	T	T
(c)	F	T	F	(d)	T	F	F

23. **Identify the following with the help of information given below.**

- **I am the second largest lake in Jammu and Kashmir.**
- **I am also called the 'Lake of Flowers'.**

Codes

(a) Loktak Lake (b) Dal Lake (c) Wular Lake (d) Kolleru Lake

Darken your choice with HB Pencil

1.	ⓐ ⓑ ⓒ ⓓ	5.	ⓐ ⓑ ⓒ ⓓ	9.	ⓐ ⓑ ⓒ ⓓ	13.	ⓐ ⓑ ⓒ ⓓ	17.	ⓐ ⓑ ⓒ ⓓ	21.	ⓐ ⓑ ⓒ ⓓ
2.	ⓐ ⓑ ⓒ ⓓ	6.	ⓐ ⓑ ⓒ ⓓ	10.	ⓐ ⓑ ⓒ ⓓ	14.	ⓐ ⓑ ⓒ ⓓ	18.	ⓐ ⓑ ⓒ ⓓ	22.	ⓐ ⓑ ⓒ ⓓ
3.	ⓐ ⓑ ⓒ ⓓ	7.	ⓐ ⓑ ⓒ ⓓ	11.	ⓐ ⓑ ⓒ ⓓ	15.	ⓐ ⓑ ⓒ ⓓ	19.	ⓐ ⓑ ⓒ ⓓ	23.	ⓐ ⓑ ⓒ ⓓ
4.	ⓐ ⓑ ⓒ ⓓ	8.	ⓐ ⓑ ⓒ ⓓ	12.	ⓐ ⓑ ⓒ ⓓ	16.	ⓐ ⓑ ⓒ ⓓ	20.	ⓐ ⓑ ⓒ ⓓ		

06

Continents and Oceans

MCQs 1 Mark Questions

1. Which continent has the largest number of population living in it?

(a) Africa (b) North America (c) Asia (d) Europe

2. The continent of North America is separated from South America by ....

(a) Suez Canal (b) Panama Canal (c) Stockholm Canal (d) Nan Madol Canal

3. Name the continent that is also known as the 'Continent of Thirsty Lands'.

(a) Asia (b) Australia (c) North America (d) Europe

4. The famous Amazon Rainforests are found in which of the following continents?

(a) Antarctica (b) South America (c) North America (d) Australia

5. Identify the continents that are completely South of the Equator.

(a) Asia and Europe (b) Australia and Antarctica

(c) North America and South America (d) Africa and Europe

6. Which continents are completely North of the Equator?

(a) North America, Europe and Asia (b) South America, Asia and Africa

(c) Australia, Africa and Antarctica (d) None of these

7. River Nile and Sahara Desert are found in ....

(a) Asia (b) Australia (c) Europe (d) Africa

8. Through which continent, both the Tropic of Cancer and Tropic of Capricorn passes?

(a) North America (b) Asia (c) Africa (d) Australia

9. Choose the incorrectly matched pair.

(a) Bird continent – South America

(b) Continent without desert – Europe

(c) Smallest continent – North America

(d) Coldest continent – Antarctica

10. In which of the following continents is Mount Everest located?
(a) Africa (b) Asia (c) Europe (d) Antarctica

11. Which of the following continents is also known as the 'new world'?
(a) North America (b) Europe (c) Asia (d) South America

12. Identify the continent that is known as the 'Peninsula of the Peninsulas'.
(a) Asia (b) Africa (c) Europe (d) South America

13. Complete the given analogy.
Deepest Ocean : Pacific Ocean :: Coldest Ocean : ?
(a) Arctic Ocean (b) Indian Ocean
(c) Atlantic Ocean (d) None of these

14. Which among the following oceans is frozen for most part of the year?
(a) Pacific Ocean (b) Atlantic Ocean (c) Indian Ocean (d) Arctic Ocean

15. What is the name of the warm ocean current that flows across the Atlantic?
(a) Labrador Current (b) Kuroshio Current
(c) California Current (d) Gulf Stream

16. Unscramble the group of letters to find out the name with the help of information given below.
It is the smallest ocean of the world.
(a) TICARC (b) NTICATLA (c) FICPACI (d) NAIDIN

17. The deepest point on the Earth, 'Mariana Trench' is located in .... ocean.
(a) Arctic (b) Indian (c) Pacific (d) Atlantic

18. Identify the name of continent, which is also known as white continent.
(a) Asia (b) Africa (c) Europe (d) Antarctica

MCQs 2 Marks Questions

19. Read the given statements and select the correct option.
I. Europe is termed as Dark Continent.
II. The name of the ocean between North America and Africa is Atlantic Ocean.
Codes
(a) Only I (b) Only II (c) Both I and II (d) Neither I nor II

20. Match the following.

List I (Continent)	List II (Mountain)
A. Asia	1. Alps
B. North America	2. Mount Albert
C. South America	3. K2
D. Europe	4. Andes

Codes

	A	B	C	D		A	B	C	D
(a)	1	2	3	4	(b)	4	3	2	1
(c)	2	4	3	1	(d)	3	2	4	1

21. On the basis of facts, some statements given below are true or false, find which ones are true (T) and which ones are false (F).

I. There are only three oceans in the world.
II. The continent of Africa has the maximum number of countries.
III. Pacific Ocean covers the largest area of the planet's surface.

Codes

	I	II	III		I	II	III
(a)	F	F	T	(b)	F	T	T
(c)	F	T	F	(d)	T	F	F

22. Identify the following with the help of information given below.

I. I am the second-largest of the world's five oceans, covering approximately one-fifth of the Earth's surface.
II. I am shaped like the letter 'S'.

(a) Arctic Ocean (b) Pacific Ocean
(c) Atlantic Ocean (d) Indian Ocean

Darken your choice with HB Pencil

1. ⓐ ⓑ ⓒ ⓓ	5. ⓐ ⓑ ⓒ ⓓ	9. ⓐ ⓑ ⓒ ⓓ	13. ⓐ ⓑ ⓒ ⓓ	17. ⓐ ⓑ ⓒ ⓓ	21. ⓐ ⓑ ⓒ ⓓ
2. ⓐ ⓑ ⓒ ⓓ	6. ⓐ ⓑ ⓒ ⓓ	10. ⓐ ⓑ ⓒ ⓓ	14. ⓐ ⓑ ⓒ ⓓ	18. ⓐ ⓑ ⓒ ⓓ	22. ⓐ ⓑ ⓒ ⓓ
3. ⓐ ⓑ ⓒ ⓓ	7. ⓐ ⓑ ⓒ ⓓ	11. ⓐ ⓑ ⓒ ⓓ	15. ⓐ ⓑ ⓒ ⓓ	19. ⓐ ⓑ ⓒ ⓓ	
4. ⓐ ⓑ ⓒ ⓓ	8. ⓐ ⓑ ⓒ ⓓ	12. ⓐ ⓑ ⓒ ⓓ	16. ⓐ ⓑ ⓒ ⓓ	20. ⓐ ⓑ ⓒ ⓓ	

07

Environment

MCQs 1 Mark Questions

1. Which of the following is the most abundant gas found in the atmosphere?
(a) Oxygen (b) Carbon dioxide (c) Nitrogen (d) Hydrogen

2. ………… present in the atmosphere obstructs harmful ultraviolet rays reaching the Earth's surface.
(a) Nitrogen (b) Carbon dioxide (c) Ozone (d) Oxygen

3. Choose amongst the following which is not a part of sphere present on the Earth.
(a) Hydrosphere (b) Atmosphere (c) Thermosphere (d) Lithosphere

4. What among of the following is not naturally present on the planet Earth?
(a) Mountains (b) Rivers (c) Oceans (d) Petrol

5. Identify the reason(s) of the changing of colour of Taj Mahal from white to yellow.
(a) Deforestation (b) Afforestation (c) Acid rain (d) All of these

6. Choose the incorrectly matched pair.
(a) Peat – Earliest type of Coal
(b) Anthracite – Hard Coal
(c) Lignite – Green Coal
(d) Bituminous – Soft Coal

7. Sound becomes hazardous noise pollution for human beings at decibels ……… .
(a) below 10 (b) below 30 (c) below 50 (d) above 70

8. Identify the poisonous gas that is present in the atmosphere.
(a) Carbon dioxide (b) Carbon monoxide
(c) Hydrogen (d) Nitrogen

9. Which among the following is/are the repercussions of the global warming?
(a) Climate change (b) Melting of glaciers
(c) Deforestation (d) Both (a) and (b)

10. **Complete the given analogy.**

Renewable sources : Hydropower :: Non-renewable sources : ?

(a) Oil (b) Natural gas (c) Coal (d) All of these

11. **Identify the non-renewable source of energy that cannot be readily replaced by natural means.**

(a) Animals (b) Forests (c) Fossil Fuels (d) Sunlight

12. **Choose amongst the following that is/are not a part of abiotic environment.**

(a) Land and water (b) Plants and animals
(c) Air (d) None of these

13. **Identify the pictures given below and choose the one for which Kaziranga National Park is famous.**

(a) 

(b) 

(c) 

(d) None of these

14. **Which of the following National Parks is known for the protection of Asiatic Lion?**

(a) Gir National Park (b) Sunderbans National Park
(c) Jim Corbett National Park (d) Ranthambhore National Park

15. **Identify from the given options, the oldest National Park of India.**

(a) Ranthambhore National Park (b) Gir National Park
(c) Kaziranga National Park (d) Sunderbans National Park

MCQs 2 Marks Questions

16. **Read the given statements and select the correct option.**

I. The ozone layer protects the species of biosphere from harmful Sun rays.

II. Water and air pollution causes death of species living in the biosphere.

Codes

(a) Only I (b) Only II (c) Both I and II (d) Neither I nor II

17. Match the following.

List I (Types of Pollution)	**List II** (Effects of Pollution)
A. Soil Pollution	1. Sleep disturbance
B. Air Pollution	2. Skin Cancer
C. Water Pollution	3. Irritation in the eyes
D. Noise Pollution	4. Jaundice

Codes

	A	B	C	D		A	B	C	D
(a)	1	2	3	4	(b)	4	1	2	3
(c)	2	3	4	1	(d)	3	1	2	4

18. On the basis of facts, some statements given below are true or false, find which ones are true (T) and which ones are false (F).

I. Lead free petrol in vehicles help in reducing pollution.

II. Using of bleach and strong detergent is one of the ways to save the Earth from getting polluted.

Codes

	I	II		I	II
(a)	F	T	(b)	T	T
(c)	F	F	(d)	T	F

19. Identify the national park with the help of information given below.

- **I am an UNESCO World Heritage Site that houses the third highest peak on the planet.**
- **I am a national park and a biosphere reserve located in Sikkim, India.**

(a) Kanchenjunga National Park (b) Keoladeo National Park

(c) Khirganga National Park (d) Kishtwar National Park

Darken your choice with HB Pencil

1.	(a) (b) (c) (d)	5.	(a) (b) (c) (d)	9.	(a) (b) (c) (d)	13.	(a) (b) (c) (d)	17.	(a) (b) (c) (d)
2.	(a) (b) (c) (d)	6.	(a) (b) (c) (d)	10.	(a) (b) (c) (d)	14.	(a) (b) (c) (d)	18.	(a) (b) (c) (d)
3.	(a) (b) (c) (d)	7.	(a) (b) (c) (d)	11.	(a) (b) (c) (d)	15.	(a) (b) (c) (d)	19.	(a) (b) (c) (d)
4.	(a) (b) (c) (d)	8.	(a) (b) (c) (d)	12.	(a) (b) (c) (d)	16.	(a) (b) (c) (d)		

08

Constitution and Government

MCQs 1 Mark Questions

1. **Who among the following has power of being the Head of Government in India?**
   (a) Chief Justice (b) Prime Minister
   (c) Home Minister (d) President

2. **What is the set of rules according to which our country is ruled called?**
   (a) Sovereignty (b) Constitution (c) Preamble (d) Fundamental Rights

3. **The defence of the country is the responsibility of which of the following governments?**
   (a) Central Government (b) State Government
   (c) Local Government (d) None of these

4. **Choose the institution(s) that is/are responsible for law making.**
   (a) Parliament (b) Supreme Court (c) High Court (d) All of these

5. **Who is the Supreme Commander of the Indian armed forces?**
   (a) Prime Minister (b) President
   (c) Council of Ministers (d) Defence Minister

6. **Identify the name of building which is shown in the image given below.**

   (a) Parliament House (b) Supreme Court of India
   (c) President House (d) North Block

7. The Vidhan Sabha and Vidhan Parishad is collectively known as ....

(a) Rajya Sabha (b) State Legislature
(c) Lok Sabha (d) None of these

8. Name the highest judicial body in the state.

(a) Supreme Court (b) High Court
(c) District Court (d) None of these

9. Which judicial body gives the final judgement in any legal case?

(a) Supreme Court of India (b) High Court
(c) District Court (d) None of these

10. For how many years, the President of India is elected?

(a) 4 (b) 5 (c) 6 (d) 2

11. Who among the following is the real head of the Indian Government?

(a) President (b) Council of Ministers
(c) Prime Minister (d) Governor

12. Identify the name of the party whose symbol is shown in the image given below.

(a) Bharatiya Janata Party (b) Aam Aadmi Party
(c) Communist Party of India (d) Indian National Congress

13. Unscramble the group of letters to find out the name with the help of information given below.

He/She is the nominated head of the state.

(a) ORNERGOV (b) IDENTPRES
(c) EMIRP RETSINIM (d) None of these

14. .... is the person who possess the executive power in the Indian Parliamentary System of government.

(a) Chief Justice (b) Home Minister
(c) Prime Minister (d) President

15. Complete the given analogy.

Village Panchayat : Rural local self-government :: Municipal Corporation : ?

(a) Central local self-government (b) Urban local self-government
(c) Government of state (d) None of these

16. Who is appointed as the real head of the state?

(a) Governor (b) Chief Minister
(c) Chief Secretary (d) None of these

17. The Lok Sabha is presided over by the ....

(a) President (b) Prime Minister
(c) Speaker (d) Government

18. Who among the following is the head of majority party in a federal government?

(a) President (b) Chief Minister
(c) Chief Justice (d) Prime Minister

19. Who is considered as the Father of the Indian Constitution?

(a) Mahatma Gandhi (b) Dr BR Ambedkar
(c) Dr S Radhakrishnan (d) Dr Rajendra Prasad

MCQs 2 Marks Questions

20. Match the following.

List I	List II
A. Democracy	1. Custodian of the Constitution
B. Supreme Court of India	2. Rule by king or queen
C. Monarchy	3. Set of principles and codes
D. Laws	4. People rule themselves through representatives

Codes

	A	B	C	D
(a)	1	2	3	4
(b)	4	1	2	3
(c)	2	4	3	1
(d)	3	1	2	4

21. Read the given statements and select the correct option.

I. The President is the head of our country.

II. The President of India should be a citizen of India.

Codes

(a) Only I

(b) Only II

(c) Both I and II

(d) Neither I nor II

22. On the basis of facts, some statements given below are true or false, find which ones are true (T) and which ones are false (F).

I. Lok Sabha is a permanent house.

II. Members of the Lok Sabha are directly elected by the people of India.

III. Lok Sabha has a Speaker and a Deputy Speaker.

Codes

	I	II	III
(a)	F	F	T
(b)	F	T	T
(c)	F	T	F
(d)	T	T	F

23. Identify the personality with the help of information given below.

I. I was a freedom fighter of independent India.

II. My first term as the Prime Minister saw the state reorganisation, India-China war, annexation of Goa amongst others.

(a) Rajendra Prasad

(b) Jawaharlal Nehru

(c) Sarvapalli Radhakrishnan

(d) Sardar Vallabhbhai Patel

Darken your choice with HB Pencil

1.	ⓐ ⓑ ⓒ ⓓ	5.	ⓐ ⓑ ⓒ ⓓ	9.	ⓐ ⓑ ⓒ ⓓ	13.	ⓐ ⓑ ⓒ ⓓ	17.	ⓐ ⓑ ⓒ ⓓ	21.	ⓐ ⓑ ⓒ ⓓ
2.	ⓐ ⓑ ⓒ ⓓ	6.	ⓐ ⓑ ⓒ ⓓ	10.	ⓐ ⓑ ⓒ ⓓ	14.	ⓐ ⓑ ⓒ ⓓ	18.	ⓐ ⓑ ⓒ ⓓ	22.	ⓐ ⓑ ⓒ ⓓ
3.	ⓐ ⓑ ⓒ ⓓ	7.	ⓐ ⓑ ⓒ ⓓ	11.	ⓐ ⓑ ⓒ ⓓ	15.	ⓐ ⓑ ⓒ ⓓ	19.	ⓐ ⓑ ⓒ ⓓ	23.	ⓐ ⓑ ⓒ ⓓ
4.	ⓐ ⓑ ⓒ ⓓ	8.	ⓐ ⓑ ⓒ ⓓ	12.	ⓐ ⓑ ⓒ ⓓ	16.	ⓐ ⓑ ⓒ ⓓ	20.	ⓐ ⓑ ⓒ ⓓ		

09

Science and Technology

MCQs 1 Mark Questions

1. Which one of the following is the strongest muscle of our body that is able to heal more quickly than other parts of the body?

(a) Tongue (b) Arms (c) Eyes (d) Legs

2. Where is the smallest bone in the human body located?

(a) Nose (b) Middle ear (c) Outer ear (d) Heel

3. Name the organ that works as an excretory and a sense organ.

(a) Lungs (b) Kidney (c) Skin (d) Ears

4. The new blood cells are made in which part of the body?

(a) Bone marrow (b) Heart (c) Kidney (d) Brain

5. Complete the given analogy.

Deficiency of Iron : Anemia :: Deficiency of Iodine : ?

(a) Rickets (b) Malnutrition (c) Goitre (d) None of these

6. The forces of attraction between the molecules are strongest in the .... state.

(a) solid (b) liquid (c) gas (d) Both (a) and (b)

7. Name the process that converts liquid to gaseous state.

(a) Condensation (b) Evaporation

(c) Boiling (d) Melting

8. Squeezing of lemon and writing in our notebooks are examples of which kinds of force?

(a) Gravitational force (b) Magnetic force

(c) Frictional force (d) Muscular force

9. Choose the incorrectly matched pair.

Types of Vitamins		**Deficiency diseases**
(a) Vitamin A	–	Night blindness
(b) Vitamin C	–	Scurvy
(c) Vitamin D	–	Brittle bones
(d) Vitamin K	–	Excessive bleeding due to injury

10. To which category does the bird shown in the image given below belong?

(a) Herbivores (b) Carnivores (c) Omnivores (d) None of these

11. Materials that allow only some light to pass through it are called ....

(a) transparent (b) translucent (c) opaque (d) semi-transparent

12. What is the name of the famous scientist who had discovered gravity?

(a) Albert Einstein (b) Isaac Newton
(c) Michael Faraday (d) None of these

13. Who among the following had given the Theory of Relativity?

(a) Isaac Newton (b) Thomas Edison
(c) Albert Einstein (d) Alexander Graham Bell

14. In which part of the body most of the digestion takes place?

(a) 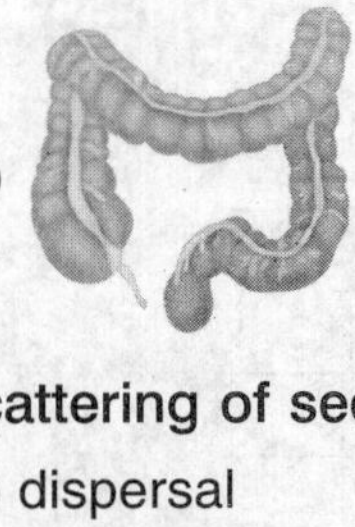 (b) 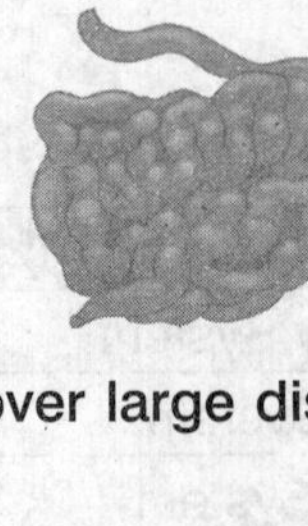 (c)  (d) 

15. Scattering of seeds over large distance is called ....

(a) dispersal (b) pollination
(c) germination (d) Both (a) and (b)

16. **Name the action that is performed when we pull our hand while touching the hot object.**

(a) Direct action (b) Involuntary action
(c) Reflex action (d) Sensory action

17. **Unscramble the group of letters to find out the correct answer with the help of information given below.**

It is the result of eating too much fatty and oily food.

(a) SITYOBE (b) HOIDTYP (c) BETESDIA (d) None of these

18. **Plants with green and soft stem like mint, rosemary are examples of ....**

(a) shrubs (b) herbs (c) climbers (d) creepers

19. **In the mountainous region, the reflection of sound arrives to the listener with a delay after the direct sound. What is it called?**

(a) Mirage (b) Echo (c) Decibel (d) None of these

20. **Which of these animals use flippers for its movement?**

(a) Lizard (b) Penguin (c) Tortoise (d) Frog

21. **Settling down of insoluble particles/solids from a mixture is known as ....**

(a) filteration (b) sedimentation (c) decantation (d) separation

22. **What is the direction of the frictional force?**

(a) At an angle (90 degree) to the direction of motion of an object.
(b) Normal to the direction of motion of an object.
(c) In the direction of an object.
(d) Opposite to the direction of motion of an object.

23. **Where is the hinge joint located in our body?**

(a) Shoulder (b) Knees (c) Ankle (d) Wrist

MCQs 2 Marks Questions

24. **Match the following.**

List I (Name of Body Parts)	**List II** (Organ System)
A. Oesophagus	1. Circulatory System
B. Heart	2. Skeleton System
C. Kidney	3. Digestive System
D. Spinal Cord	4. Excretory System

Codes

	A	B	C	D
(a)	1	2	3	4
(b)	4	1	2	3
(c)	2	4	3	1
(d)	3	1	4	2

25. **Read the given statements and select the correct option.**

I. The thick fur of polar bears keeps them warm in cold weather.

II. Birds migrate during the winter season.

Codes

(a) Only I (b) Only II (c) Both I and II (d) Neither I nor II

26. **On the basis of facts, some statements given below are true or false, find which ones are true (T) and which ones are false (F).**

I. Energy obtained from the Earth is tidal energy.

II. We get heat energy due to the burning of fuels.

III. Renewable energy can be used again and again and will never run out.

Codes

	I	II	III		I	II	III
(a)	F	T	T	(b)	T	T	T
(c)	F	T	F	(d)	T	T	F

27. **Identify the following with the help of information given below.**

- **I control the muscles and all the organs of the human body.**
- **I ensure that the heart beats properly and collects the information from the sense organs.**

(a) Blood (b) Veins (c) Skin (d) Brain

Darken your choice with HB Pencil

1.	ⓐ ⓑ ⓒ ⓓ	6.	ⓐ ⓑ ⓒ ⓓ	11.	ⓐ ⓑ ⓒ ⓓ	16.	ⓐ ⓑ ⓒ ⓓ	21.	ⓐ ⓑ ⓒ ⓓ	26.	ⓐ ⓑ ⓒ ⓓ
2.	ⓐ ⓑ ⓒ ⓓ	7.	ⓐ ⓑ ⓒ ⓓ	12.	ⓐ ⓑ ⓒ ⓓ	17.	ⓐ ⓑ ⓒ ⓓ	22.	ⓐ ⓑ ⓒ ⓓ	27.	ⓐ ⓑ ⓒ ⓓ
3.	ⓐ ⓑ ⓒ ⓓ	8.	ⓐ ⓑ ⓒ ⓓ	13.	ⓐ ⓑ ⓒ ⓓ	18.	ⓐ ⓑ ⓒ ⓓ	23.	ⓐ ⓑ ⓒ ⓓ		
4.	ⓐ ⓑ ⓒ ⓓ	9.	ⓐ ⓑ ⓒ ⓓ	14.	ⓐ ⓑ ⓒ ⓓ	19.	ⓐ ⓑ ⓒ ⓓ	24.	ⓐ ⓑ ⓒ ⓓ		
5.	ⓐ ⓑ ⓒ ⓓ	10.	ⓐ ⓑ ⓒ ⓓ	15.	ⓐ ⓑ ⓒ ⓓ	20.	ⓐ ⓑ ⓒ ⓓ	25.	ⓐ ⓑ ⓒ ⓓ		

10

Computers

MCQs 1 Mark Questions

1. **Which part of computer sends signal to other parts of the computer to tell them what to do?**

(a) Central Processing Unit (b) Motherboard
(c) Hard drive (d) Monitor

2. **Name the memory that is for short term storage and is lost when computer is turned off.**

(a) Memory Card (b) Hard Drive (c) RAM (d) Flash Drive

3. **What is the image that represents a folder or a programme called?**

(a) Application Software (b) Icon
(c) Graphic (d) All of these

4. **......... is the combination of hardware and software that facilitates the sharing of information between computing devices.**

(a) Digital device (b) Network (c) Modem (d) Computer

5. **Which among the following is an output device?**

(a) Keyboard (b) Monitor (c) Mouse (d) Scanner

6. **Complete the given analogy.**

1 byte : 8 bit :: 1024 megabytes : ?

(a) 1 GB (b) 1 MB (c) 1 KB (d) 1 TB

7. **Fifth generation computers are based on which of the following?**

(a) Bionformatics (b) Nanotechnology
(c) Programmed instruction (d) Artificial intelligence

8. **Name the pointing device that is known as touchpad, using which the cursor is moved by touching with the fingers.**

(a) Light pen (b) Track pad (c) Trackball (d) Optical Mouse

9. **What is the process of removing the unwanted part of an image called?**
(a) Hiding (b) Cropping (c) Editing (d) Formatting

10. **Which of the following is the most powerful type of computer?**
(a) Mainframe (b) Microcomputer (c) Supercomputer (d) Minicomputer

11. **Identify the given pictures and choose the device that acts as both input as well as an output device.**

(a) 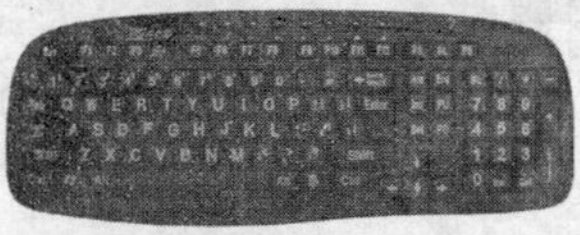

(b) 

(c) 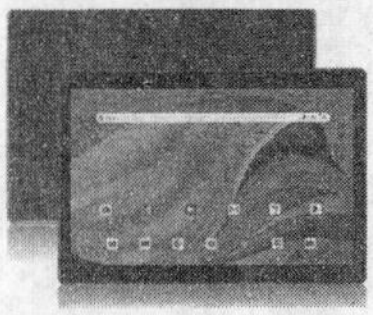

(d) 

12. **The tabs that appear at the bottom of each workbook is called ....**
(a) location tabs (b) sheet tabs (c) reference tabs (d) None of these

13. **Which of the following is used to apply centre alignment to a paragraph?**
(a) Ctrl + A (b) Ctrl + S (c) Ctrl +E (d) Ctrl + V

14. **What does CD-ROM stands for?**
(a) Compact Data Read Only Memory (b) Compact Disk Read Only Memory
(c) Compactable Disk Read Only Memory (d) Compactable Read Only Memory

15. **Which among the following is not a system software?**
(a) Windows 8 (b) Linux (c) Operating System (d) MS Word

16. **Unscramble the group of letters to find out the name with the help of information given below.**
It is another name for computer programmes and information.
(a) WARESOFT (b) WAREHARD (c) NOLOGYTECH (d) CATIONAPPLI

17. **Choose from the following options which is one of the earliest Operating System.**
(a) DOS (b) MAC (c) Windows (d) Both (a) and (b)

18. **Which among the following key is used to refresh a webpage?**
(a) F5 (b) F4 (c) F1 (d) F10

MCQs 2 Marks Questions

19. Match the following.

List I		List II
A. First Generation of Computer	1.	Transistors
B. Second Generation of Computer	2.	Integrated Circuits
C. Third Generation of Computer	3.	Micro processor
D. Fourth Generation of Computer	4.	Vacuum Tubes

Codes

	A	B	C	D		A	B	C	D
(a)	1	2	3	4	(b)	4	1	2	3
(c)	2	4	3	1	(d)	3	1	2	4

20. Read the given statements and select the correct option.

I. We can send MS Word documents to MS Excel, MS Access and MS PowerPoint.

II. Corel Draw is a software used for graphic designing.

Codes

(a) Only I (b) Only II

(c) Both I and II (d) Neither I nor II

21. On the basis of facts, some statements given below are true or false, find which ones are true (T) and which ones are false (F).

I. MS Excel produces bar charts, line graphs and pie charts.

II. Antivirus Programme is utility software.

III. Ctrl + Z command can be used to restore data immediately after the record is deleted in the Excel sheet.

Codes

	I	II	III		I	II	III
(a)	F	F	T	(b)	T	T	T
(c)	F	T	F	(d)	T	T	F

Darken your choice with HB Pencil

1.	ⓐ ⓑ ⓒ ⓓ	5.	ⓐ ⓑ ⓒ ⓓ	9.	ⓐ ⓑ ⓒ ⓓ	13.	ⓐ ⓑ ⓒ ⓓ	17.	ⓐ ⓑ ⓒ ⓓ	21.	ⓐ ⓑ ⓒ ⓓ
2.	ⓐ ⓑ ⓒ ⓓ	6.	ⓐ ⓑ ⓒ ⓓ	10.	ⓐ ⓑ ⓒ ⓓ	14.	ⓐ ⓑ ⓒ ⓓ	18.	ⓐ ⓑ ⓒ ⓓ		
3.	ⓐ ⓑ ⓒ ⓓ	7.	ⓐ ⓑ ⓒ ⓓ	11.	ⓐ ⓑ ⓒ ⓓ	15.	ⓐ ⓑ ⓒ ⓓ	19.	ⓐ ⓑ ⓒ ⓓ		
4.	ⓐ ⓑ ⓒ ⓓ	8.	ⓐ ⓑ ⓒ ⓓ	12.	ⓐ ⓑ ⓒ ⓓ	16.	ⓐ ⓑ ⓒ ⓓ	20.	ⓐ ⓑ ⓒ ⓓ		

11

General Awareness

MCQs 1 Mark Questions

Largest and Smallest in India and the World

1. **Which among the following is the biggest and coldest desert in Asia?**
(a) Thar Desert
(b) Gobi Desert
(c) Kalahari Desert
(d) None of these

2. **The largest hot desert in the world is .... desert, located in Africa.**
(a) Gibson
(b) Sahara
(c) Gobi
(d) Thar

3. **Name the deepest oceanic trench of the world.**
(a) Mariana Trench
(b) Tonga Trench
(c) Philippine Trench
(d) Kuril-Kamchatka Trench

4. **Which of the following is the largest island of the world?**
(a) Greenland
(b) Iceland
(c) Madagascar
(d) None of these

5. **Identify which among the following is the largest airport in India.**
(a) Chennai International Airport
(b) Indira Gandhi International Airport
(c) Chhatrapati Shivaji Maharaj International Airport
(d) Rajiv Gandhi International Airport

6. **......... is the biggest fish in the world.**
(a) Dolphin
(b) Star Fish
(c) Catfish
(d) Whale Shark

7. **Which among the following is the largest railway platform in the world?**
(a) Chicago Union Station, Chicago
(b) Lahore Junction, Pakistan
(c) Chhatrapati Shivaji Terminus, Mumbai
(d) Grand Central Terminal, New York

Countries, Capitals, Flags, Currencies and Language

8. Name the country that is called the 'Land of Golden Fibre'.
(a) Sri Lanka (b) Maldives
(c) Bangladesh (d) Nepal

9. Identify the country that is famous for its technological advancements.
(a) North Korea (b) South Korea
(c) China (d) Japan

10. Which of the following country's flag is similar to that of India in terms of its stripes of colours?
(a) Germany (b) France (c) Niger (d) Australia

11. The volcanic mountain Mount Vesuvius is located in which of the following countries ?
(a) Italy (b) Sweden (c) Australia (d) Norway

12. Identify the country that is popularly known as the 'Rainbow Nation'.
(a) USA (b) Japan
(c) South Africa (d) China

13. Name the country that is known as the 'The Pearl of Indian Ocean'.
(a) Myanmar (b) Sri Lanka
(c) Madagascar (d) India

14. Which of the following countries has/have its capital name same as country's name?
(a) Singapore (b) Macau
(c) Vatican City (d) All of these

15. Identify the name of country whose flag is shown in the image given below.

(a) Zimbabwe (b) Turkey (c) Canada (d) South Africa

16. Identify the incorrectly matched pair.

Country		Currency
(a) Bangladesh	–	Dhaka
(b) Israel	–	Jerusalem
(c) Mauritius	–	Port Louis
(d) Afghanistan	–	Karachi

17. Identify the currency symbol of Pakistan from the images given below.

(a)  (b)  (c)  (d) 

18. Choose the incorrectly matched pair.

Country		Currencies
(a) Belgium	–	Euro
(b) Portugal	–	Dollar
(c) Thailand	–	Baht
(d) Chile	–	Peso

19. Which of the following countries has the greatest number of official languages?

(a) China (b) India
(c) USA (d) Russia

20. Complete the given analogy.

Telugu : Andhra Pradesh :: Dogri : ?

(a) Goa (b) Jammu and Kashmir
(c) Meghalaya (d) Sikkim

21. Name the language that is the second most spoken language in India.

(a) English (b) Tamil
(c) Bengali (d) Punjabi

Cities and their Nicknames

22. Which city is also known as 'Pearl City of India'?

(a) Mumbai (b) Lucknow
(c) Bengaluru (d) Hyderabad

23. Unscramble the group of letters and find out the name with the help of information given below.

It is known as the temple city of India.

(a) PURJAI (b) RATGUJ

(c) NESWARBHUBA (d) NAUJKAN

24. Which of the following is the most populous city in the world?

(a) Delhi (b) Tokyo

(c) Beijing (d) New York

25. Name the city that is popularly known as the 'Queen of Arabian Sea'.

(a) Chennai (b) Mumbai

(c) Mussoorie (d) Kochi

26. Which city is known as the 'Silicon Valley of India' ?

(a) Bengaluru (b) Delhi (c) Mumbai (d) Kolkata

27. Name the city that is also known as 'City of Canals'.

(a) Paris (b) Amsterdam (c) Venice (d) London

Miscellaneous

28. How many states have joined together to form the United States of America?

(a) Twenty (b) Fifty (c) Ten (d) Sixty

29. Identify the tree which is associated with longevity and has important medicinal properties.

(a) Curry tree (b) Banyan tree (c) Dragon tree (d) Cacao tree

30. Identify the given pictures and choose the fastest means of transport from the given options.

(a) 

(b) 

(c) 

(d) 

31. **What is the meaning of the term 'Satyamev Jayate' mentioned on the state emblem?**

(a) Truth shall live on
(b) Only truth prevails
(c) Truth will triumph
(d) Truth will be served

32. **Identify the two rivers that combine at Devprayag to form the river Ganges.**

(a) Alaknanda and Bhagirathi River
(b) Alaknanda and Kali River
(c) Bhagirathi and Kali River
(d) None of the above

MCQs 2 Marks Questions

33. **Match the following.**

List I (Name of the Country)	**List II** (Currency Symbol)
A. Japan	1. ₽
B. Italy	2. ₤
C. United Kingdom	3. £
D. Russia	4. ¥

Codes

	A	B	C	D
(a)	1	2	3	4
(b)	4	2	3	1
(c)	2	4	3	1
(d)	3	1	2	4

34. Read the given statements and select the correct option.

I. In the Indian National Flag, saffron represents courage.

II. The horse, bull and lion are present in the National Emblem of India.

Codes

(a) Only I

(b) Only II

(c) Both I and II

(d) Neither I nor II

35. On the basis of facts, some statements given below are true or false, find which ones are true (T) and which ones are false (F).

I. The theme of World No Tobacco Day 2022 is 'Protect the Environment'.

II. Mount Everest is the highest mountain peak in the world.

III. Abu Dhabi is the capital city of Iraq.

Codes

	I	II	III
(a)	F	F	T
(b)	T	T	T
(c)	F	T	F
(d)	T	T	F

36. Identify the following with the help of information given below.

- I am called the diamond and textile city of India.
- I am located on the banks of the River Tapti near its confluence with the Arabian Sea.

(a) Kochi

(b) Surat

(c) Meerut

(d) Varanasi

Darken your choice with HB Pencil

1.	ⓐ ⓑ ⓒ ⓓ	7.	ⓐ ⓑ ⓒ ⓓ	13.	ⓐ ⓑ ⓒ ⓓ	19.	ⓐ ⓑ ⓒ ⓓ	25.	ⓐ ⓑ ⓒ ⓓ	31.	ⓐ ⓑ ⓒ ⓓ
2.	ⓐ ⓑ ⓒ ⓓ	8.	ⓐ ⓑ ⓒ ⓓ	14.	ⓐ ⓑ ⓒ ⓓ	20.	ⓐ ⓑ ⓒ ⓓ	26.	ⓐ ⓑ ⓒ ⓓ	32.	ⓐ ⓑ ⓒ ⓓ
3.	ⓐ ⓑ ⓒ ⓓ	9.	ⓐ ⓑ ⓒ ⓓ	15.	ⓐ ⓑ ⓒ ⓓ	21.	ⓐ ⓑ ⓒ ⓓ	27.	ⓐ ⓑ ⓒ ⓓ	33.	ⓐ ⓑ ⓒ ⓓ
4.	ⓐ ⓑ ⓒ ⓓ	10.	ⓐ ⓑ ⓒ ⓓ	16.	ⓐ ⓑ ⓒ ⓓ	22.	ⓐ ⓑ ⓒ ⓓ	28.	ⓐ ⓑ ⓒ ⓓ	34.	ⓐ ⓑ ⓒ ⓓ
5.	ⓐ ⓑ ⓒ ⓓ	11.	ⓐ ⓑ ⓒ ⓓ	17.	ⓐ ⓑ ⓒ ⓓ	23.	ⓐ ⓑ ⓒ ⓓ	29.	ⓐ ⓑ ⓒ ⓓ	35.	ⓐ ⓑ ⓒ ⓓ
6.	ⓐ ⓑ ⓒ ⓓ	12.	ⓐ ⓑ ⓒ ⓓ	18.	ⓐ ⓑ ⓒ ⓓ	24.	ⓐ ⓑ ⓒ ⓓ	30.	ⓐ ⓑ ⓒ ⓓ	36.	ⓐ ⓑ ⓒ ⓓ

12

Books and Authors

MCQs 1 Mark Questions

1. The book 'Seven Secrets of Shiva' is written by which famous mythologists?
(a) Amish Tripathi (b) Devdutt Pattanaik
(c) Chitra Banerjee (d) None of these

2. Who among the following was a 'Sanskrit poet' also known as the Indian Shakespeare?
(a) Kautilya (b) Kalidasa (c) Surdas (d) Tulsidas

3. The famous children's book 'Gulliver's Travels' is written by whom?
(a) Rudyard Kipling (b) George Bernard Shaw
(c) Jonathan Swift (d) Ruskin Bond

4. Choose the incorrectly matched pair.
(a) Mein Kampf – Adolf Hitler
(b) Time Machine – HG Wells
(c) Divine Comedy – Dante
(d) A Passage to India – Thomas Moore

5. Which is the only religious book ever printed in a short hand script?
(a) The Ramayana (b) The Mahabharata
(c) The Bible (d) Guru Granth Sahib

6. Complete the given analogy.
Swami and Friends : ? :: Gitanjali : Rabindranath Tagore
(a) RK Narayan (b) Shashi Tharoor (c) Vikram Seth (d) None of these

7. Name the book that is considered as the treatise on economics and politics written by Chanakya.
(a) Natyashastra (b) Arthashastra (c) Bhugolshastra (d) None of these

8. The book 'Race of My Life' is the biography of which of the following authors?
(a) Hima Das (b) Usain Bolt (c) Milkha Singh (d) Neeraj Chopra

9. **The world famous book 'The Merchant of Venice' is written by whom?**

(a) William Shakespeare (b) Thomas Moore
(c) Arthur Doyle (d) JK Rowling

10. **Choose the sportsperson who has written the autobiographical book 'Ace Against Odds'.**

(a) Mary Kom (b) Sania Nehwal (c) Sania Mirza (d) PV Sindhu

11. **Identify the given pictures and choose whose biography is 'Straight from Heart'.**

(a)  (b) 

(c)  (d) 

12. **Who among the following has written the book 'A Tale of Two Cities'?**

(a) Arthur Conan Doyle (b) Charles Dickens
(c) Thomas Moore (d) Sir Walter Scott

13. **'Far From the Madding Crowd' is written by which of the following authors?**

(a) Thomas Hardy (b) Charles Dickens
(c) William Shakespeare (d) None of these

14. **The character 'Sherlock Holmes', a famous detective, was created by whom?**

(a) JK Rowling (b) Arthur Doyle (c) Walt Disney (d) Vikram Seth

15. **The famous book 'Two States' is written by ....**

(a) Chetan Bhagat (b) Thomas Moore
(c) Arthur Doyle (d) JK Rowling

16. **Unscramble the group of letters and find out the name with the help of information given below.**

The book 'Abhigyan Shakuntalam' is written by this classical Sanskrit author.

(a) DASKALI (b) DASSUR
(c) DASTULSI (d) BARAK

17. **Name the famous Bengali fiction novel that was written by Bankim Chandra Chatterjee.**

(a) Anandamath (b) Gitanjali (c) Devdas (d) All of these

MCQs 2 Marks Questions

18. **Match the following.**

List I (Name of Author)	**List II** (Name of Books)
A. Munshi Premchand	1. Discovery of India
B. Jawaharlal Nehru	2. Malgudi Days
C. RK Narayan	3. Gaban

Codes

	A	B	C		A	B	C
(a)	1	2	3	(b)	3	2	1
(c)	2	1	3	(d)	3	1	2

19. **Read the given statements and select the correct option.**

I. The book 'David Copperfield' is written by Charles Dickens.

II. The famous book 'Animal Farm' is written by George Orwell.

Codes

(a) Only I (b) Only II (c) Both I and II (d) Neither I nor II

20. **On the basis of facts, some statements given below are true or false, find which ones are true (T) and which ones are false (F).**

I. Akbarnama is the official chronicle of the reign of Akbar, the third Mughal Emperor.

II. Antony and Cleopatra is a tragic play written by William Shakespeare.

Codes

	I	II		I	II
(a)	F	F	(b)	T	T
(c)	F	T	(d)	T	F

Darken your choice with HB Pencil

1.	ⓐ ⓑ ⓒ ⓓ	5.	ⓐ ⓑ ⓒ ⓓ	9.	ⓐ ⓑ ⓒ ⓓ	13.	ⓐ ⓑ ⓒ ⓓ	17.	ⓐ ⓑ ⓒ ⓓ
2.	ⓐ ⓑ ⓒ ⓓ	6.	ⓐ ⓑ ⓒ ⓓ	10.	ⓐ ⓑ ⓒ ⓓ	14.	ⓐ ⓑ ⓒ ⓓ	18.	ⓐ ⓑ ⓒ ⓓ
3.	ⓐ ⓑ ⓒ ⓓ	7.	ⓐ ⓑ ⓒ ⓓ	11.	ⓐ ⓑ ⓒ ⓓ	15.	ⓐ ⓑ ⓒ ⓓ	19.	ⓐ ⓑ ⓒ ⓓ
4.	ⓐ ⓑ ⓒ ⓓ	8.	ⓐ ⓑ ⓒ ⓓ	12.	ⓐ ⓑ ⓒ ⓓ	16.	ⓐ ⓑ ⓒ ⓓ	20.	ⓐ ⓑ ⓒ ⓓ

13

Important Days and Dates

MCQs 1 Mark Questions

1. **Which of the following days is celebrated as the birth anniversary of Swami Vivekananda?**

(a) National Voter's Day (b) National Youth Day
(c) Army Day (d) National Science Day

2. **Every year 'Human Rights Day' is held on ....**

(a) 5th December (b) 7th December (c) 9th December (d) 10th December

3. **Earth Day is celebrated to demonstrate support for environmental protection on which date?**

(a) 21st May (b) 22nd April (c) 2nd February (d) 14th January

4. **Choose the correctly matched pair.**

(a) National Girl Child Day – 11th October
(b) World AIDS Day – 1st December
(c) National Science Day – 5th December
(d) World Labour Day – 1st May

5. **On 13th of April every year, which historical day is observed in the memory of those who were killed in that incident?**

(a) Jallianwala Bagh Massacre Day (b) Anti-Sikh riots
(c) Great Revolt of 1857 (d) Anti-Muslim riots

6. **Which of the following dates is celebrated as the International Ozone Day designed by the United Nations General Assembly?**

(a) 16th September (b) 18th November
(c) 20th December (d) 15th January

7. **Which date is celebrated as the World Heritage Day to promote awareness about the cultural heritage and diversity on the planet?**

(a) 18th April (b) 10th March (c) 13th February (d) 2nd January

8. **Complete the given analogy.**
Hiroshima Day : 6th August :: Nagasaki Day : ?
(a) 5th September (b) 9th August (c) 10th July (d) 19th June

9. **When is the World Water Day celebrated worldwide?**
(a) 8th March (b) 22nd March (c) 14th October (d) 19th January

10. **World Health Day is a global health awareness day celebrated every year on which date?**
(a) 7th April (b) 9th April (c) 12th April (d) 20th April

11. **Every Year 'World Peace Day' is celebrated by the United Nations on ....**
(a) 1st January (b) 2nd January (c) 21st September (d) 5th January

12. **The National Sports Day is celebrated in India as a tribute to Major Dhyan Chand. When is it celebrated?**
(a) 29th August (b) 30th August (c) 31st August (d) 1st September

13. **When is the International Day of Non-Violence is observed?**
(a) 1st October (b) 2nd October (c) 3rd October (d) 4th October

14. **Identify the given pictures and select from the following that is celebrated on 11th October across the world.**

(a) 

(b) 

(c) 

(d) None of these

MCQs 2 Marks Questions

15. **Read the given statements and select the correct option.**
I. **'National Science Day' is celebrated in India as a tribute to CV Raman.**
II. **'World Heart Day' is celebrated every year on 29th September to spread awareness about Heart Health.**

Codes

(a) Only I (b) Only II (c) Both I and II (d) Neither I nor II

16. Match the following.

List I	List II
A. World Laughter Day	1. 10th January
B. Indian Army Day	2. 15th January
C. World Cancer Day	3. 4th February

Codes

	A	B	C		A	B	C
(a)	1	2	3	(b)	3	1	2
(c)	2	3	1	(d)	3	1	2

17. On the basis of facts, some statements given below are true or false, find which ones are true (T) and which ones are false (F).

I. International Women's Day is observed on 8th February.

II. International Day of Happiness is held on 20th March.

III. On 1st January, World Peace Day is celebrated worldwide.

Codes

	I	II	III		I	II	III
(a)	F	F	T	(b)	T	T	T
(c)	F	T	F	(d)	T	T	F

18. Identify the following with the help of information given below.

- **I am celebrated every year on 3rd March as according to the UN General Assembly resolution.**
- **I am celebrated to raise awareness of the world's wild fauna and flora.**

(a) World Wildlife Day (b) International World Ecosystem Day

(c) World Forest Day (d) World Environment Day

Darken your choice with HB Pencil

1.	ⓐ ⓑ ⓒ ⓓ	4.	ⓐ ⓑ ⓒ ⓓ	7.	ⓐ ⓑ ⓒ ⓓ	10.	ⓐ ⓑ ⓒ ⓓ	13.	ⓐ ⓑ ⓒ ⓓ	16.	ⓐ ⓑ ⓒ ⓓ
2.	ⓐ ⓑ ⓒ ⓓ	5.	ⓐ ⓑ ⓒ ⓓ	8.	ⓐ ⓑ ⓒ ⓓ	11.	ⓐ ⓑ ⓒ ⓓ	14.	ⓐ ⓑ ⓒ ⓓ	17.	ⓐ ⓑ ⓒ ⓓ
3.	ⓐ ⓑ ⓒ ⓓ	6.	ⓐ ⓑ ⓒ ⓓ	9.	ⓐ ⓑ ⓒ ⓓ	12.	ⓐ ⓑ ⓒ ⓓ	15.	ⓐ ⓑ ⓒ ⓓ	18.	ⓐ ⓑ ⓒ ⓓ

14

Awards - National and International

MCQs 1 Mark Questions

1. **Who was the first Asian (Indian) to receive the Nobel Prize?**
   (a) Rabindranath Tagore
   (b) CV Raman
   (c) Amartya Sen
   (d) Mother Teresa

2. **Which is the second highest Military Award in India that is given for the acts of evident gallantry in the presence of the enemy?**
   (a) Vir Chakra
   (b) Maha Vir Chakra
   (c) Param Vir Chakra
   (d) None of these

3. **Who among the following was the first Indian woman to receive Nobel Peace Prize?**
   (a) Kasturba Gandhi
   (b) Indira Gandhi
   (c) Mother Teresa
   (d) None of these

4. **Identify the name of award which is shown in the image given below.**

   (a) IIFA Award
   (b) Grammy Award
   (c) Jnanpith Award
   (d) Param Vir Chakra

5. Choose the incorrectly matched pair.

(a) Arjuna Award – Sports and Games
(b) Grammy Award – Music Industry
(c) Jnanpith Award – Drama and Acting
(d) Academy Award – Film Industry

6. Padma Vibhushan and Padma Shri Awards are given on which of the following events?

(a) Republic Day (b) Independence Day
(c) Vijay Diwas (d) Gandhi Jayanti

7. Identify who was/were the first recipients of Bharat Ratna Award in 1954.

(a) CV Raman (b) Sarvepalli Radhakrishnan
(c) C Rajagopalachari (d) All of these

8. Which ministry confers the Major Dhyan Chand Award that is the lifetime achievement sporting honour of the Republic of India?

(a) Ministry of Youth Affairs and Sports
(b) Ministry of Human Resource
(c) Ministry of Commerce
(d) None of the above

9. Choose the highest Military Award that is awarded for the gallantry on the battlefield.

(a) Param Vir Chakra (b) Ashoka Chakra
(c) Maha Vir Chakra (d) None of these

10. Identify the field in which the 'Nobel Prizes' are not awarded.

(a) Physics and Chemistry (b) Language and Economics
(c) Peace and Social Work (d) Music and Mathematics

11. Who among the following selects the awardees for Padma Awards?

(a) President of India
(b) Prime Minister of India
(c) A selected committee for the award
(d) Both (a) and (b)

12. Which of the following is India's highest peace time gallantry award?

(a) Maha Vir Chakra (b) Vir Chakra
(c) Ashoka Chakra (d) Param Vir Chakra

13. Identify from the given options, the literary award that India's National Academy of Letters, annually confers on writers of the most outstanding books of literary merit.

(a) Sahitya Akademi Award
(b) Saraswati Samman
(c) Bhasha Samman
(d) Premchand Fellowship

14. Choose an annual award hosted to honour the best British and international contributions to film.

(a) The Academy Awards
(b) BAFTA
(c) Film Fare Awards
(d) None of these

15. Name the award for achievements in newspaper, magazine, online journalism, literature and musical composition within the United States.

(a) Pulitzer Prize
(b) Booker Prize
(c) Nobel Prize
(d) None of these

MCQs 2 Marks Questions

16. Match the following.

List I	List II
A. Shaurya Chakra	1. Civilian Award
B. Padma Bhushan	2. Military Award
C. Dronacharya Award	3. Bravery Award
D. Sarvottam Jeevan Raksha Padak	4. Sports Award

Codes

	A	B	C	D
(a)	1	2	3	4
(b)	4	1	2	3
(c)	2	1	4	3
(d)	3	1	2	4

17. Read the given statements and select the correct option.

I. Rajiv Gandhi Khel Ratna Award is the highest honour given in sports.

II. This award is given to the best Coach in India.

Codes

(a) Only I

(b) Only II

(c) Both I and II

(d) Neither I nor II

18. On the basis of facts, some statements given below are true or false, find which ones are true (T) and which ones are false (F).

I. The International Gandhi Peace Prize, named after Mahatma Gandhi, is awarded annually by the Government of India.

II. The Nari Shakti Puraskar is an annual award given by the Ministry of Women and Child Development.

III. Indira Gandhi Prize for Peace, Disarmament and Development, is the prestigious award accorded annually by Indira Gandhi Memorial Trust.

Codes

	I	II	III
(a)	F	F	T
(b)	T	T	T
(c)	F	T	F
(d)	T	T	F

Darken your choice with HB Pencil

1. ⓐ ⓑ ⓒ ⓓ	4. ⓐ ⓑ ⓒ ⓓ	7. ⓐ ⓑ ⓒ ⓓ	10. ⓐ ⓑ ⓒ ⓓ	13. ⓐ ⓑ ⓒ ⓓ	16. ⓐ ⓑ ⓒ ⓓ
2. ⓐ ⓑ ⓒ ⓓ	5. ⓐ ⓑ ⓒ ⓓ	8. ⓐ ⓑ ⓒ ⓓ	11. ⓐ ⓑ ⓒ ⓓ	14. ⓐ ⓑ ⓒ ⓓ	17. ⓐ ⓑ ⓒ ⓓ
3. ⓐ ⓑ ⓒ ⓓ	6. ⓐ ⓑ ⓒ ⓓ	9. ⓐ ⓑ ⓒ ⓓ	12. ⓐ ⓑ ⓒ ⓓ	15. ⓐ ⓑ ⓒ ⓓ	18. ⓐ ⓑ ⓒ ⓓ

15

Sports

MCQs 1 Mark Questions

1. What do the five rings in an Olympic flag represent?
(a) Five games (b) Five colours
(c) Five countries (d) Five continents

2. Which among the following is the governing body for the sport of Archery?
(a) World Archery Federation (b) World Archery Association
(c) World Archery Council (d) Archery Federation of the World

3. Identify the sports personality who had become the first Grandmaster from India.
(a) Soumya Swaminathan (b) Viswanathan Anand
(c) Abhijeet Gupta (d) Tania Sachdev

4. Choose from the following the shape of a Basketball court.
(a) Oval (b) Square (c) Rectangular (d) Circular

5. Identify the incorrectly matched pair.

Name of Cricket Stadium		Location
(a) Wankhede Stadium	–	Mumbai
(b) Sardar Patel Stadium	–	Gandhi Nagar
(c) Eden Gardens	–	Kolkata
(d) Arun Jaitley Stadium	–	Delhi

6. Who is the first Indian woman to win Asian games Gold in 400m run?
(a) Kamaljeet Sandhu (b) Dutee Chand
(c) Tintu Luka (d) Rita Sen

7. Name the sportsperson who has been nicknamed as 'Dhing Express'.
(a) Swapna Barman (b) Hima Das
(c) PT Usha (d) Dutee Chand

8. Who was the first Indian Badminton player to hold number one rank in world ranking?

(a) Saina Nehwal (b) Prakash Padukone
(c) Chetan Anand (d) PV Sindhu

9. First Asian Games was held in .... city.

(a) Jakarta (b) Beijing (c) Tokyo (d) New Delhi

10. Durand Cup and Grey Cup are associated with which sport?

(a) Hockey (b) Badminton (c) Football (d) Lawn Tennis

11. Identify the sportsperson who is shown in the image given below.

(a) Geeta Phogat (b) Harmanpreet Kaur
(c) Priyanka Phogat (d) Ritu Phogat

12. Complete the given analogy.

Sania Mirza : Tennis : : PV Sindhu : ?

(a) Badminton (b) Chess (c) Cricket (d) Hockey

13. Serena Williams is one of the top ranked sportswomen of ....

(a) Table tennis (b) Tennis (c) Badminton (d) Golf

14. How many members are there on each side of a Kabaddi match?

(a) 5 (b) 7 (c) 6 (d) 8

15. Which among the following countries has won the ICC World Cup the most number of times?

(a) Sri Lanka (b) India (c) Australia (d) South Africa

16. Who among the following Indian players, won the first Olympic Gold in shooting?

(a) Abhinav Bindra (b) Gagan Narang
(c) Jitu Rai (d) None of these

17. Identify the yogasana shown in the picture given below.

(a) Halasana (b) Uttanasana
(c) Balasana (d) Ustrasana

18. Which of the following terms is not associated with Football?

(a) Catch (b) Penalty Kick
(c) Off Side (d) Penalty Stroke

19. Identify the given pictures and choose the correct image that shows 'Bhujangasana' (yoga poses).

(a) 

(b) 

(c) 

(d) 

20. Who among the following is/are allowed to touch the ball with his feet during a Hockey match?

(a) Defender (b) Centre- forward
(c) Goal Keeper (d) All of these

21. Which of the following stadiums is associated with Hockey?

(a) Eden Garden Stadium (b) Sardar Patel Stadium
(c) Dhyan Chand Stadium (d) Nehru Stadium

MCQs 2 Marks Questions

22. Match the following.

List I (Name of the Country)	**List II** (National Sports)
A. USA	1. Table Tennis
B. United Kingdom	2. Bull Fighting
C. Spain	3. Baseball
D. China	4. Cricket

Codes

	A	B	C	D		A	B	C	D
(a)	1	2	3	4	(b)	4	1	2	3
(c)	2	3	4	1	(d)	3	4	2	1

23. Read the given statements and select the correct option.

I. Saina Nehwal has won India's first Olympic Medal in Badminton.

II. Maria Sharapova is a Russian Badminton player and also an Olympic medalist.

Codes

(a) Only I
(b) Only II
(c) Both I and II
(d) Neither I nor II

On the basis of facts, some statements given below are true or false, find which ones are true (T) and which ones are false (F).

I. India won the first Cricket World Cup in the year in 1983.

II. Neeraj Chopra is a track and field athlete from India who competes in the Javelin Throw.

III. Abhijeet Kunte is related to the game to Chess.

Codes

	I	II	III		I	II	III
(a)	F	F	T	(b)	T	T	T
(c)	F	T	F	(d)	T	T	F

Darken your choice with HB Pencil

1. ⓐ ⓑ ⓒ ⓓ	5. ⓐ ⓑ ⓒ ⓓ	9. ⓐ ⓑ ⓒ ⓓ	13. ⓐ ⓑ ⓒ ⓓ	17. ⓐ ⓑ ⓒ ⓓ	21. ⓐ ⓑ ⓒ ⓓ
2. ⓐ ⓑ ⓒ ⓓ	6. ⓐ ⓑ ⓒ ⓓ	10. ⓐ ⓑ ⓒ ⓓ	14. ⓐ ⓑ ⓒ ⓓ	18. ⓐ ⓑ ⓒ ⓓ	22. ⓐ ⓑ ⓒ ⓓ
3. ⓐ ⓑ ⓒ ⓓ	7. ⓐ ⓑ ⓒ ⓓ	11. ⓐ ⓑ ⓒ ⓓ	15. ⓐ ⓑ ⓒ ⓓ	19. ⓐ ⓑ ⓒ ⓓ	23. ⓐ ⓑ ⓒ ⓓ
4. ⓐ ⓑ ⓒ ⓓ	8. ⓐ ⓑ ⓒ ⓓ	12. ⓐ ⓑ ⓒ ⓓ	16. ⓐ ⓑ ⓒ ⓓ	20. ⓐ ⓑ ⓒ ⓓ	24. ⓐ ⓑ ⓒ ⓓ

16

First in India and the World

MCQs 1 Mark Questions

1. **Who was the first person to reach the peak of Mount Everest?**

(a) Edmund Hillary (b) Michael Brown
(c) Nawang Lutuk (d) Pemba Dorje

2. **The first country to host the modern Olympic Games was ....**

(a) USA (b) Greece (c) India (d) Russia

3. **Paper was first invented in which of the following countries?**

(a) Japan (b) China (c) USA (d) Germany

4. **Who was the first woman to receive the Bharat Ratna?**

(a) Pratibha Patil (b) Indira Gandhi (c) Mother Teresa (d) Lata Mangeshkar

5. **Which among the following was the first country to print a book?**

(a) China (b) Japan (c) Russia (d) USA

6. **Identify the woman who was chosen as the first Miss World from India.**

(a) Priyanka Chopra (b) Reita Faria
(c) Manushi Chhillar (d) Sushmita Sen

7. **Choose the incorrectly matched pair.**

(a) First Indian in Space – Rakesh Sharma
(b) First Vice-President of India – Dr Radhakrishnan
(c) First woman Chief Minister of India – Indira Gandhi
(d) First Law and Justice Minister of India – BR Ambedkar

8. **Name the lady who became the first female IPS officer of India.**

(a) Kanchan Chaudhary Bhattacharya (b) Priya Ravichandran
(c) Kalpana Saxena (d) Kiran Bedi

9. Complete the given analogy.

First woman Governor of India : Sarojini Naidu :: First woman Chief Justice of High Court : ?

(a) Leela Seth (b) Annie Besant (c) Sushma Chawla (d) None of these

10. The first country to prepare a written Constitution was ....

(a) Greece (b) USA (c) United Kingdom (d) India

11. Name the first person to sail around the world.

(a) Marco Polo (b) Magellan (c) Columbus (d) None of these

12. Which is the first country to launch artificial satellite in the space?

(a) Russia (b) China (c) Japan (d) UK

13. Unscramble the group of letters to find out the correct answer with the help of information given below.

It is the first shuttle to go into space.

(a) BIACOLUM (b) BHATTARYA

(c) OLOAPP (d) None of these

14. Name the first woman President of the United Nations General Assembly.

(a) Vijaya Lakshmi Pandit (b) Margaret Thatcher

(c) Sirimavo Bandaranaike (d) None of these

15. Which was the first space craft to reach on Mars?

(a) Gaganyan (b) Viking I (c) Columbia (d) Insight

16. Who among the following became the first woman pilot in Indian Navy?

(a) Astha Sehgal (b) Roopa A

(c) Sakthi Maya S (d) Shubhangi Swaroop

MCQs 2 Marks Questions

17. Match the following.

List I	List II
A. First person to reach North Pole	1. Yuri Gagarin
B. First man to fly into space	2. Junko Tabei
C. First woman to climb Mount Everest	3. Robert Peary

Codes

	A	B	C		A	B	C
(a)	1	2	3	(b)	3	2	1
(c)	2	3	1	(d)	3	1	2

18. Read the given statements and select the correct option.

I. The first Indian man to have climbed Mount Everest was Avatar Singh.

II. The first Governor General of free India was Lord Mountbatten.

Codes

(a) Only I (b) Only II
(c) Both I and II (d) Neither I nor II

19. On the basis of facts, some statements given below are true or false, find which ones are true (T) and which ones are false (F).

I. The first British Governor General of India was Lord William Bentick.

II. The first Prime Minister of free India was Rajendra Prasad.

III. The first and the last Indian to be Governor General of free India was C Rajgopalachari.

Codes

	I	II	III		I	II	III
(a)	F	F	T	(b)	T	F	T
(c)	F	T	F	(d)	T	T	F

20. Identify the following with the help of information given below.

- **I was the first person to win the Magsaysay Award in 1958.**
- **I am considered as the National Teacher of India and often referred to as Acharya.**

(a) Vinoba Bhave
(b) Mahatma Gandhi
(c) Jawaharlal Nehru
(d) S Radhakrishnan

Darken your choice with HB Pencil

1.	ⓐ ⓑ ⓒ ⓓ	5.	ⓐ ⓑ ⓒ ⓓ	9.	ⓐ ⓑ ⓒ ⓓ	13.	ⓐ ⓑ ⓒ ⓓ	17.	ⓐ ⓑ ⓒ ⓓ
2.	ⓐ ⓑ ⓒ ⓓ	6.	ⓐ ⓑ ⓒ ⓓ	10.	ⓐ ⓑ ⓒ ⓓ	14.	ⓐ ⓑ ⓒ ⓓ	18.	ⓐ ⓑ ⓒ ⓓ
3.	ⓐ ⓑ ⓒ ⓓ	7.	ⓐ ⓑ ⓒ ⓓ	11.	ⓐ ⓑ ⓒ ⓓ	15.	ⓐ ⓑ ⓒ ⓓ	19.	ⓐ ⓑ ⓒ ⓓ
4.	ⓐ ⓑ ⓒ ⓓ	8.	ⓐ ⓑ ⓒ ⓓ	12.	ⓐ ⓑ ⓒ ⓓ	16.	ⓐ ⓑ ⓒ ⓓ	20.	ⓐ ⓑ ⓒ ⓓ

Practice Set 01

Time : 60 Mins.

Max. Marks : 60

General Instructions

1. This question paper contains 50 questions.
2. All questions are compulsory. There is no negative marking.
3. This question paper is divided into two parts; In first part, there are 40 MCQs of 1 mark each while in second part, there are 10 MCQs of 2 marks each.
4. Use HB pencil / Blue ball point pen to mark your choice of answer by darkening the circles on the OMR Sheet.

MCQs 1 Mark Questions

1. Who built the famous Sanchi Stupa in Madhya Pradesh?

(a) Ashoka
(b) Chandragupta Maurya
(c) Bindusara
(d) Kanishka

2. Which of the following is also known as Black pagoda?

(a) Sun Temple, Konark
(b) Dwarkadhish Temple, Gujarat
(c) Jagannath Temple
(d) Khajuraho Temple

3. Asteroids are found in the belt between Mars and ....

(a) Jupiter
(b) Saturn
(c) Uranus
(d) Earth

4. Who among the following was the first Indian pilot?

(a) Sardar Baldev Singh
(b) JRD Tata
(c) Sardar Vallabhbhai Patel
(d) RK Shanmukham Chetty

5. Complete the given analogy.

Kathak : Uttar Pradesh : : Mohiniyattam : ?

(a) Kerala
(b) Tamil Nadu
(c) Karnataka
(d) Andhra Pradesh

6. The famous Khajuraho Temple is located in ....

(a) Madhya Pradesh
(b) Rajasthan
(c) Gujarat
(d) Andhra Pradesh

7. President is the supreme commander of which among the following?

(a) Army
(b) Navy
(c) Air Force
(d) All of these

8. Choose the name of country whose flag is shown in the image given below.

(a) United Kingdom (b) Greece
(c) Sweden (d) Canada

9. What is the name of the tallest brick and stone minarets that is located in New Delhi?

(a) Jama Masjid (b) Taj Mahal (c) Qutub Minar (d) Humayun's Tomb

10. Complete the given analogy.
Valmiki : Ramayana : : Ved Vyasa : ?

(a) Mahabharata (b) Rig Veda (c) Panchatantra (d) Dharmasutra

11. Which of the following terms is not associated with football?

(a) Catch (b) Penalty kick
(c) Off side (d) Penalty Stroke

12. Who among the following gave the slogan "Swaraj is my Birthright and I shall have it"?

(a) Lala Lajpat Rai (b) Bal Gangadhar Tilak
(c) Bhagat Singh (d) Subhash Chandra Bose

13. Lignite is also known by which of the following names?

(a) Black Coal (b) White Coal (c) Red Coal (d) Green Coal

14. Unscramble the group of letters to find out the correct answer with the help of information given below.
The movement of the Earth around the Sun on a fixed path or orbit is called ....

(a) TIONMO (b) TIONROTA (c) TIONLUREVO (d) None of these.

15. Which among the following are separated by Panama Canal?

(a) Asia and Europe (b) Asia and Australia
(c) North America and South America (d) South America and Africa

16. Identify the name of trench which is present in Pacific Ocean.

(a) Java Trench (b) Mariana Trench (c) Puerto Rico Trench (d) All of these

17. From the pictures given below identify the animal for which Gir National Park is famous.

(a) 

(b) 

(c) 

(d) 

18. Who amongst the following is the head of State Government?

(a) Governor (b) Chief Justice of High Court
(c) Chief Minister (d) Council of Ministers

19. Tea leaves can be separated from the tea by the process of ....

(a) filtration (b) sedimentation (c) evaporation (d) sublimation

20. Peso is the currency of which country?

(a) Argentina (b) Chile (c) Japan (d) China

21. Identify the name of lake which is the deepest lake in the world.

(a) Wular Lake (b) Baikal Lake (c) Dal Lake (d) Chilika Lake

22. Odisha is associated with Rath Yatra of which of the following?

(a) Lord Balbhadra (b) Lord Jagannath
(c) Goddess Subhadra (d) All of these

23. Gallantry Awards and Padma Awards are conferred on which of the following occasions?

(a) Independence Day (b) Republic Day
(c) Gandhi Jayanti (d) Good Governance Day

24. Deficiency of which of the following leads to anaemia?

(a) Iron (b) Iodine (c) Vitamin D (d) Protein

25. Who among the following is credited with the founding of Microsoft?

(a) Bill Gates (b) Tim Cook (c) Elon Musk (d) Steve Jobs

26. Identify the sportsperson who is known in the image given below.

(a) Sandesh Jhingam (b) Abhinav Bindra
(c) Anirudh Thapa (d) Gurpreet Singh Sandhu

27. Lala Lajpat Rai belonged to which state?

(a) Punjab (b) Maharashtra (c) West Bengal (d) Bihar

28. Identify the incorrectly matched pair.

(a) Renewable resource – Water
(b) Non-Renewable resource – Coal
(c) Biotic component – River
(d) Abiotic component – Mountains

29. Which of the following is the largest freshwater lake of world?

(a) Superior Lake (b) Victoria Lake
(c) Mansarovar Lake (d) Caspian Sea

30. From the given options which government building(s) is/are located in New Delhi?

(a) Parliament (b) Rashtrapati Bhawan
(c) Supreme Court of India (d) All of these

31. National Youth Day is celebrated on the birth anniversary of whom amongst the following?

(a) Swami Vivekananda (b) Atal Bihari Vajpayee
(c) Subhash Chandra Bose (d) Lala Lajpat Rai

32. Which of the following days is celebrated on the occasion of birth anniversary of Homi Bhabha?

(a) National Science Day (b) National Space Day
(c) National Nuclear Day (d) National Engineer's Day

33. Identify the vitamin that helps in strengthening our immune system.

(a) Vitamin C (b) Vitamin D (c) Vitamin A (d) Vitamin B

34. **Which among the following is not a software?**

(a) Microsoft Word (b) Microsoft Excel
(c) Microsoft Windows (d) Microsoft Paint

35. **Who amongst the following was the first woman Chief Minister of India?**

(a) Sarojini Naidu (b) Sucheta Kriplani
(c) Indira Gandhi (d) Usha Mehta

36. **Identify the planet which is also known as Twin sister of the Earth.**

(a) Mercury (b) Venus (c) Mars (d) Jupiter

37. **Identify the book that is not written by APJ Abdul Kalam.**

(a) Ignited Minds (b) Wings of Fire
(c) Turning Points (d) Passage to India

38. **Japan is also known as ....**

(a) Land of Midnight Sun (b) Land of Rising Sun
(c) Land of Dark Continent (d) None of these

39. **Identify the field in which Jnanpith Award is given.**

(a) Music Industry (b) Literary
(c) Film Industries (d) Sports and Games

40. **Which date is celebrated as the World Heritage Day to promote awareness about the cultural heritage and diversity on the planet?**

(a) 18th April (b) 10th March
(c) 13th February (d) 2nd January

MCQs 2 Marks Questions

41. **Match the following.**

	List I	List II
A.	Hornbill Festival	1. Nagaland
B.	Hemis Festival	2. Ladakh
C.	Losar Festival	3. Arunachal Pradesh
D.	Onam	4. Kerala

Codes

	A	B	C	D		A	B	C	D
(a)	1	2	3	4	(b)	2	1	4	3
(c)	3	4	1	2	(d)	4	3	2	1

42. Consider the following statements and choose the correct ones.

I. Babur was the founder of Mughal Empire in India.

II. Jama Masjid and Red Fort were built during the rule of Shah Jahan.

III. Buland Darwaza was built by Akbar.

Codes

(a) Only I (b) II and III (c) I and II (d) All of these

43. On the basis of facts, some statements given below are true or false, find which ones are true (T) and which ones are false (F).

I. India Gate is the highest entrance gate in the world.

II. Indian Museum which is the oldest museum is located in Mumbai.

III. Jaisalmer Fort is also known as Great Wall of India.

Codes

	I	II	III		I	II	III
(a)	T	T	T	(b)	F	F	F
(c)	F	T	T	(d)	T	T	F

44. Consider the following statements and choose incorrect ones from the codes given below.

I. Venus has lesser rotation time than the Earth.

II. Group of stars that forms patterns is known as constellations.

III. Stars do not have their own light.

Codes

(a) I and II (b) II and III (c) I and III (d) I, II and III

45. Identify the river with the help of information given below.

- It is the major river of India which drains into Bay of Bengal.
- It is formed due to confluence of Alaknanda and Bhagirathi.

(a) Ganga (b) Godavari (c) Yamuna (d) Saraswati

46. Identify the continent with the help of information given below.

- It is also known as the Continent of Thirsty Lands.
- It is located in the Southern hemisphere and is the smallest continent.

(a) Antarctica (b) Australia (c) Asia (d) Europe

47. Read the following statements and choose the correct option.

I. Icon is the image that represents the folder or a programme.

II. F5 key is used to refresh the page.

III. CTRL+S is used to used to save the document.

(a) I and II (b) II and III (c) I and III (d) I, II and III

48. Match the following.

	List I	List II
A.	Defence	1. Central Government
B.	Law Making	2. Parliament
C.	Panchayati Raj	3. Local Government
D.	Lok Sabha	4. Lower House

Codes

	A	B	C	D		A	B	C	D
(a)	1	2	3	4	(b)	2	1	4	3
(c)	3	2	1	4	(d)	4	3	1	2

49. On the basis of facts, some statements given below are true or false, find which ones are true (T) and which ones are false (F).

I. Hima Das is known as 'Dhing Express'.

II. India was the winner of first T20 world cup held in 2007.

III. Neeraj Chopra is the player associated with Discuss Throw.

Codes

	I	II	III		I	II	III
(a)	F	T	T	(b)	T	T	F
(c)	F	F	F	(d)	T	T	T

50. Identify the person with the help of information given below.

- He is also known as Indian Shakespeare.
- He is the Author of the famous play 'Shakuntala' and 'Meghdoot'.

(a) Kalidasa (b) Soordas (c) Kabir (d) Ashwaghosha

Darken your choice with HB Pencil

1.	ⓐ ⓑ ⓒ ⓓ	10.	ⓐ ⓑ ⓒ ⓓ	19.	ⓐ ⓑ ⓒ ⓓ	28.	ⓐ ⓑ ⓒ ⓓ	37.	ⓐ ⓑ ⓒ ⓓ	46.	ⓐ ⓑ ⓒ ⓓ
2.	ⓐ ⓑ ⓒ ⓓ	11.	ⓐ ⓑ ⓒ ⓓ	20.	ⓐ ⓑ ⓒ ⓓ	29.	ⓐ ⓑ ⓒ ⓓ	38.	ⓐ ⓑ ⓒ ⓓ	47.	ⓐ ⓑ ⓒ ⓓ
3.	ⓐ ⓑ ⓒ ⓓ	12.	ⓐ ⓑ ⓒ ⓓ	21.	ⓐ ⓑ ⓒ ⓓ	30.	ⓐ ⓑ ⓒ ⓓ	39.	ⓐ ⓑ ⓒ ⓓ	48.	ⓐ ⓑ ⓒ ⓓ
4.	ⓐ ⓑ ⓒ ⓓ	13.	ⓐ ⓑ ⓒ ⓓ	22.	ⓐ ⓑ ⓒ ⓓ	31.	ⓐ ⓑ ⓒ ⓓ	40.	ⓐ ⓑ ⓒ ⓓ	49.	ⓐ ⓑ ⓒ ⓓ
5.	ⓐ ⓑ ⓒ ⓓ	14.	ⓐ ⓑ ⓒ ⓓ	23.	ⓐ ⓑ ⓒ ⓓ	32.	ⓐ ⓑ ⓒ ⓓ	41.	ⓐ ⓑ ⓒ ⓓ	50.	ⓐ ⓑ ⓒ ⓓ
6.	ⓐ ⓑ ⓒ ⓓ	15.	ⓐ ⓑ ⓒ ⓓ	24.	ⓐ ⓑ ⓒ ⓓ	33.	ⓐ ⓑ ⓒ ⓓ	42.	ⓐ ⓑ ⓒ ⓓ		
7.	ⓐ ⓑ ⓒ ⓓ	16.	ⓐ ⓑ ⓒ ⓓ	25.	ⓐ ⓑ ⓒ ⓓ	34.	ⓐ ⓑ ⓒ ⓓ	43.	ⓐ ⓑ ⓒ ⓓ		
8.	ⓐ ⓑ ⓒ ⓓ	17.	ⓐ ⓑ ⓒ ⓓ	26.	ⓐ ⓑ ⓒ ⓓ	35.	ⓐ ⓑ ⓒ ⓓ	44.	ⓐ ⓑ ⓒ ⓓ		
9.	ⓐ ⓑ ⓒ ⓓ	18.	ⓐ ⓑ ⓒ ⓓ	27.	ⓐ ⓑ ⓒ ⓓ	36.	ⓐ ⓑ ⓒ ⓓ	45.	ⓐ ⓑ ⓒ ⓓ		

Practice Set 02

Time : 60 Mins. Max. Marks : 60

General Instructions

1. This question paper contains 50 questions.
2. All questions are compulsory. There is no negative marking.
3. This question paper is divided into two parts; In first part, there are 40 MCQs of 1 mark each while in second part, there are 10 MCQs of 2 marks each.
4. Use HB pencil / Blue ball point pen to mark your choice of answer by darkening the circles on the OMR Sheet.

MCQs 1 Mark Questions

1. CV Raman received the Nobel Prize in which field?

(a) Physics (b) Mathematics (c) Economics (d) Peace

2. The famous book .... was written by Chetan Bhagat.

(a) Seven Secrets of Shiva (b) Wings of Fire
(c) Two States (d) Ignited Minds

3. Identify the games that were hosted by Greece for the first time?

(a) Asian Games (b) Commonwealth Games
(c) FIFA World Cup (d) Modern Olympic Games

4. What was the earlier name of Chhatrapati Shivaji Maharaj Terminus?

(a) Mumbai Central (b) Hazrat Nizamuddin
(c) Victoria Terminus (d) Lokamanya Tilak Terminus

5. Choose the continent among the following that lies in the Northern Hemisphere.

(a) Africa (b) Europe (c) North America (d) All of these

6. Identify the personality, who is shown in the image given below.

(a) Nocolous Copernicus (b) Charles Darwin
(c) Thomas Edison (d) Micheal Faraday

7. Which fair is famous in Gujarat held annually as a festival?

(a) Trade Fair (b) Rann Utsav

(c) Ganga Sagar Mela (d) Pushkar Mela

8. Complete the given analogy.

Divine Comedy : ? :: The Namesake : Jhumpa Lahiri

(a) Amitav Ghosh (b) Dante

(c) Devdatt Patnaik (d) Chetan Bhagat

9. Tsangpo is also known by which river in India?

(a) Godavari (b) Brahmaputra (c) Ganga (d) Yamuna

10. When is the Birth Anniversary of Lal Bahadur Shastri celebrated?

(a) 2nd September (b) 2nd October (c) 2nd December (d) 12th October

11. .... is the result of eating too much fatty and oily food.

(a) Diabetes (b) Obesity (c) Typhoid (d) Diarrhea

12. Identify from given pictures, the leader who introduced the concept of Swaraj.

(a) 

(b) 

(c) 

(d) 

13. Who amongst the following is not related to Tennis?

(a) Sania Mirza (b) Pullela Gopichand

(c) Mahesh Bhupathi (d) Leander Paes

14. Which among the following monuments is turning yellow due to the Acid Rain?

(a) Red Fort (b) Bibi Ka Makbara (c) Taj Mahal (d) Victoria memorial

15. Lala Lajpat Rai was also known by the name of ....

(a) Punjab Kesari (b) Bihar Kesari

(c) Lion of West Bengal (d) Maharashtra Kesari

16. Choose the incorrectly matched pair.

(a) Kumbh Mela – Ujjain
(b) Nauchandi Mela – Meerut
(c) Hampi – Karnataka
(d) Ugadi – Bihar

17. Unscramble the group of letters to find out the correct option with the help of Information given below.

India's most haunted place 'Bhangarh Fort' is located in this state.

(a) JASRATHAN (b) RASHMAHTRAA (c) KHANJHARD (d) TAKANAKAR

18. Identify the first Indian woman who receive Nobel Peace Prize.

(a) Indira Gandhi (b) Mother Teresa (c) Kasturba Gandhi (d) Neena Gupta

19. Choose the odd one out.

(a) Scanner (b) Joystick (c) Printer (d) Windows

20. Who amongst the following known as Father of Indian Renaissance?

(a) Raja Ram Mohan Roy (b) Jawaharlal Nehru
(c) Sardar Patel (d) Khan Abdul Gaffar Khan

21. Identify the state in which Dudhsagar falls are located.

(a) Goa (b) Karnataka (c) Maharashtra (d) Odisha

22. How many rings are represented on the flag of Olympics?

(a) 5 (b) 7 (c) 3 (d) 6

23. Which country is also known as Land of Midnight Sun?

(a) Norway (b) Sweden (c) Africa (d) France

24. The Rajya Sabha is presided over by the ....

(a) Parliament (b) President (c) Chief Minister (d) Vice-President

25. Identify the name of country whose currency is shown in image given below.

(a) Africa (b) Japan (c) Australia (d) China

26. Identify the name of first woman who became the pilot in Indian Navy.

(a) Sucheta Kripalani (b) Shubhangi Swaroop
(c) Junko Tabei (d) Margaret Thatcher

27. The picture given below is of Reita Faria. Which of the following titles was won by her?

(a) First woman to win Miss Universe from India
(b) First woman to win Miss India
(c) First Woman to win Miss World from India
(d) First woman to win Nobel Prize in Physics

28. Identify the tab which appear at the bottom of each workbook.

(a) Location Tab (b) Reference Tab (c) Sheet Tab (d) None of these

29. Which planet is also known as ringed planet?

(a) Saturn (b) Jupiter (c) Uranus (d) Mars

30. Identify the theory which was given by Albert Einstein.

(a) Theory of Gravity (b) Theory of Relativity
(c) Theory of Evolution (d) Atomic Theory

31. Arun Jaitley stadium is located in which city of India?

(a) Chandigarh (b) Nagpur (c) New Delhi (d) Kolkata

32. The period between day and night is called as ....

(a) Orbit (b) Dusk (c) Axis (d) Dawn

33. Identify the name of tiger reserve, which is located in the state of West Bengal.

(a) Periyar Tiger Reserve (b) Sundarban Tiger Reserve
(c) Bandipur Tiger Reserve (d) Sariska National Park

34. Our country is governed according to the set of rules known as ....

(a) Constitution (b) Charter (c) Sovereignty (d) Preamble

35. **Which among the following is the largest fort in India and a world Heritage Site?**
(a) Agra Fort (b) Chittorgarh Fort (c) Charminar Fort (d) Kumbhalgarh Fort

36. **Identify the country that is famous for its technoloigal advancements.**
(a) China (b) Japan (c) South Korea (d) Russia

37. **Which continent is also known as Bird Continent?**
(a) North America (b) South America (c) Asia (d) Africa

38. **Identify the non-renewable source of energy from the options given below.**
(a) Natural gas (b) Nuclear energy
(c) Hydrocarbon gas (d) All of these

39. **Which date is famously celebrated as World Labour Day?**
(a) 11th October (b) 25th December (c) 1st February (d) 1st May

40. **Identify the image that is shown in picture given below.**

(a) Orbit (b) Meteors (c) Asteroids (d) Comets

MCQs 2 Marks Questions

41. **Match the following.**

	List I		List II
(a)	Param Vir Chakra	1.	Military
(b)	Arjuna Award	2.	Sports
(c)	Academy Award	3.	Acting
(d)	Dhanvantri Award	4.	Medicine

Codes

	A	B	C	D		A	B	C	D
(a)	1	2	3	4	(b)	2	1	4	3
(c)	3	4	2	1	(d)	4	3	1	2

42. Read the following statements and choose the correct option.

I. Kumbha Mela is one of the biggest Hindu festivals that is celebrated four times over the course of 12 years.

II. Gangaur is the traditional festival of Rajasthan.

III. The themes of Bharatnatyam Dance are taken from Mahabharata and Ramayana.

Codes

(a) I and II (b) II and III (c) I and III (d) I, II and III

43. On the basis of facts, some statements given below are true or false, find which ones are true (T) and which ones are false (F).

I. The Book Ignited Minds is authored by Jawaharlal Nehru.

II. Ramayana is the only religious book ever printed in short hand script.

III. Gulliver's Travels is written by Charles Dickens.

Codes

	I	II	III		I	II	III
(a)	T	T	T	(b)	F	F	F
(c)	F	T	T	(d)	T	F	F

44. Identify the architecture with the help of information given below.

- It is the oldest stone structure in India.
- It was built by Mauryan Emperor Ashoka the Great.

(a) Sanchi Stupa (b) Red Fort
(c) Sarnath Pillar (d) Vijay Stambh

45. Identify the river with the help of information given below.

I. It is the largest tributary of Ganga River.

II. It confluences with Ganga River at Prayagraj in Uttar Pradesh.

(a) Godavari (b) Yamuna (c) Kaveri (d) Krishna

46. Read the following statements and choose the incorrect option.

I. Sushma Chawla has been elected as the first Woman Chief Justice of High Court.

II. India is the first country to have a written Constitution.

III. Margaret Thatcher was the first Woman President of United Nations Assembly.

Codes

(a) I and II (b) II and III (c) I and III (d) I, II and III

47. Match the following.

List I	List II
A. Output Device	1. Monitor
B. Input Device	2. Keyboard
C. Software	3. MS Office
D. Bar below the computer screen	4. Taskbar

Codes

	A	B	C	D		A	B	C	D
(a)	1	2	3	4	(b)	2	1	4	3
(c)	3	4	2	1	(d)	4	3	1	2

48. Identify the continent with the help of information given below.

- It is also known as Dark Continent.
- Tropic of Cancer and Tropic of Capricorn passes through this continent.

(a) Africa (b) America (c) Asia (d) Oceania

49. Read the given statements and select the correct option.

I. Saturn is the hottest planet in the Solar System.

II. Mercury is the second farthest planet from the Sun.

Codes

(a) Only I (b) Only II (c) Both I and II (d) Neither I nor II

50. Identify the following with the help of information given below.

- I am located on the banks of the River Tapti near its confluence with the Arabian Sea.
- I am also known as the Green City of India.

(a) Varanasi (b) Kochi (c) Surat (d) Meerut

Darken your choice with HB Pencil

1.	ⓐ ⓑ ⓒ ⓓ	10.	ⓐ ⓑ ⓒ ⓓ	19.	ⓐ ⓑ ⓒ ⓓ	28.	ⓐ ⓑ ⓒ ⓓ	37.	ⓐ ⓑ ⓒ ⓓ	46.	ⓐ ⓑ ⓒ ⓓ
2.	ⓐ ⓑ ⓒ ⓓ	11.	ⓐ ⓑ ⓒ ⓓ	20.	ⓐ ⓑ ⓒ ⓓ	29.	ⓐ ⓑ ⓒ ⓓ	38.	ⓐ ⓑ ⓒ ⓓ	47.	ⓐ ⓑ ⓒ ⓓ
3.	ⓐ ⓑ ⓒ ⓓ	12.	ⓐ ⓑ ⓒ ⓓ	21.	ⓐ ⓑ ⓒ ⓓ	30.	ⓐ ⓑ ⓒ ⓓ	39.	ⓐ ⓑ ⓒ ⓓ	48.	ⓐ ⓑ ⓒ ⓓ
4.	ⓐ ⓑ ⓒ ⓓ	13.	ⓐ ⓑ ⓒ ⓓ	22.	ⓐ ⓑ ⓒ ⓓ	31.	ⓐ ⓑ ⓒ ⓓ	40.	ⓐ ⓑ ⓒ ⓓ	49.	ⓐ ⓑ ⓒ ⓓ
5.	ⓐ ⓑ ⓒ ⓓ	14.	ⓐ ⓑ ⓒ ⓓ	23.	ⓐ ⓑ ⓒ ⓓ	32.	ⓐ ⓑ ⓒ ⓓ	41.	ⓐ ⓑ ⓒ ⓓ	50.	ⓐ ⓑ ⓒ ⓓ
6.	ⓐ ⓑ ⓒ ⓓ	15.	ⓐ ⓑ ⓒ ⓓ	24.	ⓐ ⓑ ⓒ ⓓ	33.	ⓐ ⓑ ⓒ ⓓ	42.	ⓐ ⓑ ⓒ ⓓ		
7.	ⓐ ⓑ ⓒ ⓓ	16.	ⓐ ⓑ ⓒ ⓓ	25.	ⓐ ⓑ ⓒ ⓓ	34.	ⓐ ⓑ ⓒ ⓓ	43.	ⓐ ⓑ ⓒ ⓓ		
8.	ⓐ ⓑ ⓒ ⓓ	17.	ⓐ ⓑ ⓒ ⓓ	26.	ⓐ ⓑ ⓒ ⓓ	35.	ⓐ ⓑ ⓒ ⓓ	44.	ⓐ ⓑ ⓒ ⓓ		
9.	ⓐ ⓑ ⓒ ⓓ	18.	ⓐ ⓑ ⓒ ⓓ	27.	ⓐ ⓑ ⓒ ⓓ	36.	ⓐ ⓑ ⓒ ⓓ	45.	ⓐ ⓑ ⓒ ⓓ		

Answer Sheet

Chapter 01

1. (c)	**2.** (a)	**3.** (b)	**4.** (d)	**5.** (b)	**6.** (b)	**7.** (a)	**8.** (b)	**9.** (c)	**10.** (c)
11. (b)	**12.** (c)	**13.** (a)	**14.** (b)	**15.** (b)	**16.** (a)	**17.** (c)	**18.** (c)	**19.** (c)	**20.** (b)
21. (c)									

Chapter 02

1. (b)	**2.** (a)	**3.** (c)	**4.** (a)	**5.** (c)	**6.** (b)	**7.** (b)	**8.** (b)	**9.** (a)	**10.** (a)
11. (a)	**12.** (c)	**13.** (a)	**14.** (b)	**15.** (c)	**16.** (c)	**17.** (b)	**18.** (a)		

Chapter 03

1. (b)	**2.** (a)	**3.** (b)	**4.** (b)	**5.** (a)	**6.** (c)	**7.** (b)	**8.** (c)	**9.** (a)	**10.** (b)
11. (b)	**12.** (b)	**13.** (a)	**14.** (a)	**15.** (a)	**16.** (a)	**17.** (a)	**18.** (d)	**19.** (b)	**20.** (a)
21. (b)	**22.** (d)	**23.** (b)	**24.** (a)						

Chapter 04

1. (b)	**2.** (b)	**3.** (c)	**4.** (c)	**5.** (d)	**6.** (b)	**7.** (c)	**8.** (a)	**9.** (b)	**10.** (b)
11. (a)	**12.** (a)	**13.** (a)	**14.** (a)	**15.** (b)	**16.** (d)	**17.** (b)	**18.** (a)	**19.** (b)	**20.** (c)
21. (c)	**22.** (c)	**23.** (b)	**24.** (b)	**25.** (c)	**26.** (a)	**27.** (b)	**28.** (a)	**29.** (d)	**30.** (b)
31. (b)									

Chapter 05

1. (c)	**2.** (b)	**3.** (c)	**4.** (a)	**5.** (c)	**6.** (d)	**7.** (c)	**8.** (d)	**9.** (d)	**10.** (b)
11. (c)	**12.** (b)	**13.** (d)	**14.** (a)	**15.** (b)	**16.** (d)	**17.** (a)	**18.** (d)	**19.** (b)	**20.** (b)
21. (c)	**22.** (b)	**23.** (b)							

Chapter 06

1. (c)	**2.** (b)	**3.** (b)	**4.** (b)	**5.** (b)	**6.** (a)	**7.** (d)	**8.** (c)	**9.** (c)	**10.** (b)
11. (a)	**12.** (c)	**13.** (a)	**14.** (d)	**15.** (d)	**16.** (a)	**17.** (c)	**18.** (d)	**19.** (b)	**20.** (d)
21. (b)	**22.** (c)								

Chapter 07

1. (c)	**2.** (c)	**3.** (c)	**4.** (d)	**5.** (c)	**6.** (c)	**7.** (d)	**8.** (a)	**9.** (d)	**10.** (d)
11. (c)	**12.** (b)	**13.** (a)	**14.** (a)	**15.** (c)	**16.** (c)	**17.** (c)	**18.** (d)	**19.** (a)	

Chapter 08

1. (b)	**2.** (b)	**3.** (a)	**4.** (a)	**5.** (b)	**6.** (b)	**7.** (b)	**8.** (b)	**9.** (a)	**10.** (b)
11. (c)	**12.** (c)	**13.** (b)	**14.** (d)	**15.** (b)	**16.** (b)	**17.** (c)	**18.** (d)	**19.** (b)	**20.** (b)
21. (c)	**22.** (b)	**23.** (b)							

Chapter 09

1. (a)	**2.** (b)	**3.** (c)	**4.** (a)	**5.** (c)	**6.** (a)	**7.** (b)	**8.** (d)	**9.** (c)	**10.** (b)
11. (b)	**12.** (b)	**13.** (c)	**14.** (b)	**15.** (a)	**16.** (c)	**17.** (a)	**18.** (a)	**19.** (b)	**20.** (b)
21. (b)	**22.** (d)	**23.** (b)	**24.** (d)	**25.** (c)	**26.** (a)	**27.** (d)			

Chapter 10

1. (a)	**2.** (c)	**3.** (b)	**4.** (b)	**5.** (b)	**6.** (a)	**7.** (d)	**8.** (b)	**9.** (b)	**10.** (c)
11. (c)	**12.** (b)	**13.** (c)	**14.** (b)	**15.** (d)	**16.** (a)	**17.** (a)	**18.** (a)	**19.** (b)	**20.** (c)
21. (b)									

Chapter 11

1. (b)	**2.** (b)	**3.** (a)	**4.** (a)	**5.** (b)	**6.** (d)	**7.** (d)	**8.** (c)	**9.** (d)	**10.** (c)
11. (a)	**12.** (d)	**13.** (b)	**14.** (d)	**15.** (b)	**16.** (d)	**17.** (c)	**18.** (b)	**19.** (b)	**20.** (b)
21. (c)	**22.** (d)	**23.** (c)	**24.** (b)	**25.** (d)	**26.** (a)	**27.** (c)	**28.** (b)	**29.** (b)	**30.** (c)
31. (c)	**32.** (a)	**33.** (b)	**34.** (c)	**35.** (d)	**36.** (b)				

Chapter 12

1. (b)	**2.** (b)	**3.** (c)	**4.** (d)	**5.** (c)	**6.** (a)	**7.** (b)	**8.** (a)	**9.** (a)	**10.** (c)
11. (b)	**12.** (b)	**13.** (a)	**14.** (b)	**15.** (a)	**16.** (a)	**17.** (a)	**18.** (d)	**19.** (c)	**20.** (b)

Chapter 13

1. (b)	**2.** (d)	**3.** (b)	**4.** (d)	**5.** (a)	**6.** (a)	**7.** (a)	**8.** (b)	**9.** (b)	**10.** (a)
11. (c)	**12.** (a)	**13.** (b)	**14.** (a)	**15.** (c)	**16.** (a)	**17.** (b)	**18.** (a)		

Chapter 14

1. (a)	**2.** (b)	**3.** (c)	**4.** (b)	**5.** (c)	**6.** (a)	**7.** (d)	**8.** (a)	**9.** (a)	**10.** (d)
11. (c)	**12.** (c)	**13.** (a)	**14.** (b)	**15.** (a)	**16.** (c)	**17.** (a)	**18.** (b)		

Chapter 15

1. (d)	**2.** (a)	**3.** (b)	**4.** (c)	**5.** (b)	**6.** (a)	**7.** (b)	**8.** (b)	**9.** (b)	**10.** (c)
11. (b)	**12.** (a)	**13.** (b)	**14.** (b)	**15.** (c)	**16.** (a)	**17.** (a)	**18.** (a)	**19.** (a)	**20.** (c)
21. (c)	**22.** (d)	**23.** (a)	**24.** (b)						

Chapter 16

1. (a)	**2.** (b)	**3.** (b)	**4.** (b)	**5.** (a)	**6.** (b)	**7.** (c)	**8.** (d)	**9.** (a)	**10.** (b)
11. (b)	**12.** (a)	**13.** (a)	**14.** (a)	**15.** (b)	**16.** (d)	**17.** (d)	**18.** (c)	**19.** (b)	**20.** (a)

Practice Set 01

1. (a)	**2.** (a)	**3.** (a)	**4.** (b)	**5.** (a)	**6.** (a)	**7.** (d)	**8.** (c)	**9.** (c)	**10.** (a)
11. (a)	**12.** (b)	**13.** (d)	**14.** (c)	**15.** (c)	**16.** (b)	**17.** (a)	**18.** (a)	**19.** (a)	**20.** (b)
21. (b)	**22.** (b)	**23.** (b)	**24.** (a)	**25.** (a)	**26.** (b)	**27.** (a)	**28.** (c)	**29.** (d)	**30.** (d)
31. (a)	**32.** (d)	**33.** (a)	**34.** (c)	**35.** (b)	**36.** (b)	**37.** (d)	**38.** (b)	**39.** (b)	**40.** (a)
41. (a)	**42.** (d)	**43.** (b)	**44.** (c)	**45.** (a)	**46.** (b)	**47.** (d)	**48.** (a)	**49.** (b)	**50.** (a)

Practice Set 02

1. (a)	**2.** (c)	**3.** (d)	**4.** (c)	**5.** (d)	**6.** (b)	**7.** (b)	**8.** (b)	**9.** (b)	**10.** (b)
11. (b)	**12.** (d)	**13.** (b)	**14.** (c)	**15.** (a)	**16.** (d)	**17.** (a)	**18.** (b)	**19.** (d)	**20.** (a)
21. (a)	**22.** (a)	**23.** (a)	**24.** (d)	**25.** (d)	**26.** (b)	**27.** (a)	**28.** (c)	**29.** (a)	**30.** (b)
31. (c)	**32.** (b)	**33.** (b)	**34.** (a)	**35.** (b)	**36.** (b)	**37.** (b)	**38.** (d)	**39.** (d)	**40.** (d)
41. (a)	**42.** (d)	**43.** (b)	**44.** (a)	**45.** (b)	**46.** (d)	**47.** (a)	**48.** (a)	**49.** (d)	**50.** (c)